Creating Winning Bids

Basil Sawczuk

RIBA Publishing

© Basil Sawczuk, 2013

Published by RIBA Publishing, 15 Bonhill Street, London EC2P 2EA

ISBN 978 1 85946 498 4
Stock code 80354

The right of Basil Sawczuk to be identified as the Author of this Work has been asserted in accordance with the Copyright, Design and Patents Act 1988.

British Library Cataloguing in Publications Data

A catalogue record for this book is available from the British Library.

Commissioning Editor: James Thompson
Project Editor: Neil O'Regan
Designed and typeset by Academic + Technical
Printed and bound by W.G. Baird, Antrim

While every effort has been made to check the accuracy and quality of the information given in this publication, neither the Author nor the Publisher accept any responsibility for the subsequent use of this information, for any errors or omissions that it may contain, or for any misunderstandings arising from it.

RIBA Publishing is part of RIBA Enterprises Ltd.
www.ribaenterprises.com

Contents

CHAPTER 1 FINDING OPPORTUNITIES TO BID FOR WORK   **1**

Not so daunting   1

Bidding to win work   1

Understanding the bidding process   3

Types of bid   5

Ways to make a bid   7

E-procurement and e-auctions   10

Bidding through procurement agencies   11

CHAPTER 2 WHAT TO ESTABLISH BEFORE TENDER OR PRE-QUALIFICATION RELEASE   **13**

The need for background information   13

Things to know before the documentation is received   13

CHAPTER 3 CREDIBILITY, CAPABILITY, COMPATIBILITY AND RELIABILITY (THE 3Cs + R TEST)   **27**

The 3Cs + R test   27

Credibility   27

Capability   30

Compatibility   31

Reliability   34

Reasons why bids fail and the need to obtain feedback   34

'Bid or no bid' decision   38

How good is your relationship?   38

Increase your chances of success   39

CHAPTER 4 IMPROVING YOUR CHANCES OF SUCCESS THROUGH BETTER UNDERSTANDING OF YOUR COMPETITORS   **43**

Is there a favourite already?   43

How to win if there is a favourite   44

If there is an incumbent, focus on the service gap   44

What to do if you are the incumbent   45

continued

Compare yourself to the competition		47
Differentiate yourself from your competitors to increase your chances of success		49
Differentiate through customer service		50
Maximising your strengths and subtly revealing the weaknesses in your competition		51

CHAPTER 5	**PREPARATION AND PLANNING THE PROCESS**	**53**
	Timetable and process	53
	Contributors and team selection	53
	Keep the prospective client involved	53
	Process for preparing the document	54
	Process, revision and reviews	55
	Themes and winning strategy	57
	Format and production	57

CHAPTER 6	**CREATING THE DOCUMENT**	**63**
	The seven-step checklist on content – the 'must have' elements	63
	Step 1: Write the content to address the evaluation criteria	63
	Step 2: Do you pass the 'so what?' test (all about features and benefits)	63
	Step 3: Address all the issues the client may have	69
	Step 4: Use the client's language	70
	Step 5: See your answer from the client's point of view	73
	Step 6: Create a reason to select your proposal	74
	Step 7: Be compliant	74
	Writing an executive summary	75
	Principles of clear writing	75
	Avoid being sidetracked when writing	76
	Structuring the answer	76
	Layout and style	77
	Patterns, signposts and bridges	79
	Using lists, tables and graphics	80

CHAPTER 7	**USING APPENDICES**	**83**
	When to use an appendix	83
	Make an appendix appropriate	85
	Format	85
	Content	86
	Example of an appendix	86

CHAPTER 8	**SHOWING OFF PAST PROJECTS**	**89**
	The need to demonstrate skills, experience and capability	89
	The need for a knowledge bank	90
	The use of project stamps, mini project profiles, project profiles and case studies to illustrate a point	93
	Format and content	97

CHAPTER 9	**OTHER CONSIDERATIONS**	**101**
	Incorporating third party endorsements	101
	Supplying client references	105
	Using CVs	105

| | **INDEX** | **111** |

Dedication

To Sonia and Luke.

About the Author

Basil Sawczuk runs Potentialise, a consultancy advising small and large firms on how best to secure profitable work.

Soon after qualifying as an architect Basil found he was becoming very successful in securing new business. Recognising this, his colleagues encouraged him to be a full time job-winner, handing over to others to be in charge of project delivery.

His career has included securing projects for many blue-chip clients both in the UK and abroad for the multi-professional firm DGI International, working as Marketing Director for WS Atkins Property Services, incorporating three divisions selling and marketing architects, civil, structural and building services engineers, quantity surveyors and facilities management, and operating out of more than fifty UK offices. Basil has also been a Marketing Director of a regional law firm, and Marketing, Business Development and Bid Director for a major contractor focusing mainly on outsourced public sector work. He is also a visiting lecturer to several universities, a speaker at conferences, seminars and training workshops. He can be contacted on basil@potentialise.com

CHAPTER 1
Finding opportunities to bid for work

Not so daunting

For a small consultancy it might seem quite daunting to start bidding for work. There are so many opportunities available that it is often difficult to know where to start and how to deal with new opportunities as they arise.

This guide takes you through the many types of opportunities that exist and sets out how to quickly evaluate those that are most likely to be successful for you. Once you have decided which bid to pursue, the first step is to identify the key points that the potential client is looking for, then consider how best to address these points to improve your chances of securing the project. The guide details how to plan the process of bid preparation, how to create the document, how to incorporate your experience and additional information within the main body of the submission and how to use appendices creatively and effectively.

First, we will consider what is required to successfully bid for work, scrutinising the process and explaining some of the jargon that is used in the bidding process. Then we will detail the types of bid and the various ways in which a bid can be made.

One word of caution is needed here: this guide provides an approach to creating compelling winning bids but does not deal with the contractual aspects. You may need to take advice from lawyers, advisers and professional indemnity (PI) insurance providers when entering into a contractual relationship with clients.

Bidding to win work

When starting up a consultancy, the opportunities for new commissions will probably come through existing relationships, recommendations and perhaps as a result of some form of marketing. As the firm grows and the portfolio of completed projects increases, the consultancy's credibility will be enhanced and the opportunities to successfully bid for more work will increase. The ability to use your past experience and current resources to increase your workload makes bidding for work both exciting and rewarding.

In the past, work was awarded on the basis of existing relationships, especially in the private sector; however, there is now a trend towards clients becoming more selective. As a result, most clients will use some form of bidding process to:

- reduce the risk of making the wrong choice
- satisfy shareholders (or the public if the work is in the public sector) that the selection process was fair
- achieve value for money
- select a consultant whose ethos matches their culture
- ensure that the consultants are financially stable, have sufficient resources, appropriate experience and the necessary systems and technology in place to suit the demands of the project
- obtain input from the consultants at an early stage.

Given this trend, more and more opportunities are available through some form of bidding process. To improve the chances of success, some investment of time must be made to gather information that will be required in the bidding process. However, once this initial effort has been made and sufficient information gathered in presentable formats, it becomes a matter of simply reworking the data for subsequent bids.

Many small consultancies believe that bidding for work in a competitive environment is only for the bigger consultancies. This is not true. Some major private sector clients have smaller projects available where a smaller consultancy, with fewer overheads, could have a better chance of winning the work. Also, virtually all work placed by the public sector, regardless of value, has to go through some form of bidding process. The smaller, lower value projects may be particularly attractive to smaller firms.

Most consultancies will be experienced in submitting proposals. Proposals tend to be a response to a discussion with a potential client, where the client asks for some information to assist them in the decision-making process. The temptation in this situation is to send the client a brochure or other general information. However, this may not prove sufficient to secure the work, especially if competitors are able to produce more bespoke and compelling proposals. Therefore, knowing how to produce a compelling bid will also dramatically increase your success rate when submitting a proposal in a situation where there is no bidding process.

So, what does it take to successfully bid for work? Listed below are a few attributes that would certainly help:

Enthusiasm	Clients tend to buy from enthusiastic people. They want to be inspired and reassured that they have made the right choice. Enthusiasm should be evident in your writing and when meeting the client during the pre-bid or bidding process.

Ability to understand the client's needs	To stand a good chance of winning a bid you must be able to convince the client that, not only do you understand their needs, but that you are also able to deliver the appropriate service to suit those needs. There should be clear ambition on your part to establish exactly what the client wants. Chapter 2 looks at the 25 things you need to know before the bid documentation is issued. A small practice might find it difficult to devote adequate resources to this process, but once the correct client management procedures are put in place, then this process becomes more achievable.
Being realistic about your ability to win	If you don't know the client and there is no relationship between you, then you really have to consider the probability of successfully bidding for the project. Also, if you have limited resources then you should be very selective in the bids that you pursue. Don't attempt too many bids or target projects for which you are not suited.
Commitment	It is important to emphasise that preparing a compelling and winning bid is not easy and requires time and effort. There are no short cuts.
Determination	If, at first, you are not successful then don't give up. Obtain feedback from the client and improve the next bid accordingly.
Good writing skills	Being able to communicate in a clear, unambiguous way is essential. Use positive and persuasive language.
Time and process management	Most bidding opportunities have some form of time constraints for the various stages. There must therefore be an internal process in place to coordinate the efforts of all the parties that may be contributing to the bid. In addition, you will need to manage your own time carefully in order to properly address the bid within the imposed deadlines.

Understanding the bidding process

Many consultancies, especially smaller firms, are deterred from bidding for work because they do not fully understand the process involved. This is understandable as there is no standard bid process. Large, complex projects, by their very nature, may have a long process with many stages. Smaller projects, however, might involve a simple exchange of letters.

Where public money is involved, UK projects must adhere to European Union (EU) procurement laws and there are set procedures that must be followed. These procedures vary depending on the value of the contract.

It is worthwhile taking some time to understand the bidding process and considering whether it is worth expressing an interest. In simple terms, the bidding process could follow the following sequence:

Contract notice	The client may advertise the project in trade magazines or in the *Official Journal of the European Union* (*OJEU*).
Expression of interest (EOI)	The contract notice will ask interested parties to submit an EOI. This might involve providing contact details. In the public sector it may be necessary to provide some additional information at this stage.
Pre-qualification questionnaire (PQQ)	This is a questionnaire issued by the client that asks for information to assist in the shortlisting process. This usually covers finance, experience, health and safety, equal opportunities, environmental policies and additional information about the business.
Evaluation	The client, or their advisers, will evaluate the PQQ, usually against pre-set criteria and a scoring matrix.
Invitation to tender (ITT)	Those shortlisted will be sent the tender documentation and will be invited to submit a tender. The documentation will probably include a letter of invitation, instructions to tenderers, a description of services required, pricing document, terms and conditions and a pre-addressed envelope for returning the bid.
Tender submission	This is the submission of the tender documentation.
Tender evaluation	The award of the tender may be based purely on the tender submission or may also include, and be influenced by, an interview or presentation, a visit to other projects completed by the tenderer and a period of negotiation.
Two-stage tender	On larger projects there may be a further shortlisting stage during the tender process. This is usual if the tender process is expensive for those bidding. After the initial tender submission, the client may continue discussions with, say, the best two tenderers and request a further, more detailed and worked-up submission. This is sometimes referred to as a best and final offer (BAFO).
Contract award	This is the formality of appointing the tenderer.

Types of bid

Negotiated contract

If you have a good existing relationship with the client, you might not be involved in a competitive bid process but would instead negotiate the contract. This may still require some form of bid documentation. In these situations you should consider the following points:

- Take the time and effort to submit a good proposal, ensuring that your suitability for the project is beyond question – don't give the client a reason to seek an alternative proposal.
- Refresh your existing relationship – don't let the client think that you are taking the relationship for granted. Deal with your existing client as if they were a new client that you are trying to convince to appoint you.
- Enhance your service offering – your client might have been approached by your competitors and they may be offering better value for money.
- Obtain feedback whenever you can – emphasise the good points in your proposals or bid and demonstrate how you have addressed any shortcomings.

Bidding direct to the client
Single project

A private sector client has a degree of flexibility in terms of the format and procedure of the bidding process. Public sector projects within the EU, however, have to comply with set procedures.

The procedure for public sector projects is primarily determined by the project value. If the value of a project is below a certain threshold, then the procedure is more relaxed. Smaller consultancies may wish to target these lower value projects and there are a number of websites that list these opportunities. The website www.supply2.gov.uk is a good starting point to find low-value public sector opportunities. It is free for local searches but a fee applies to regional or national searches. The Tenders Electronic Daily (TED) website lists all the public sector projects above the value threshold.

Where a project is above the value threshold, then the public sector client may opt for one of the following:

Restricted tender process	The consultant (service provider) will have to respond to an advertisement expressing an interest in tendering. They will then have to complete a PQQ to demonstrate that they have sufficient experience and resources to meet the client's needs. Only those who are subsequently shortlisted and invited may submit a tender.

Open tender process	This differs from the restricted tender process in that all those who request the tender documentation will be invited to submit a tender. There is no shortlisting with a PQQ stage. Instead, the information that is normally requested in the PQQ is requested as part of the tender. This procedure is often used if the timetable does not permit the separate PQQ stage or the marketplace is limited and the client wishes to stimulate extra interest.
Negotiated tender process	This uses a PQQ stage but allows the client to negotiate the contract terms within strict guidelines. This process is rarely used and is usually confined to exceptional circumstances, such as when a rapid response is required in emergencies or where a particular company is the sole provider of supply, or relevant experience or capability.

Therefore, when bidding for a single project direct to the client, consider:

- targeting the private sector where the process may be simpler and involve less red tape
- that there may be an opportunity to negotiate without the need for competitive bids in the private sector, which is rarely the case in the public sector
- targeting the low-value projects within the public sector where there may be limited competition from larger competitors. Equally, if you are a larger consultancy then perhaps you would not be able to compete on price against the smaller competitors who may be targeting the lower value work.

Framework contracts

In a framework contract or framework agreement, the client has a programme of work over a period of time and agrees in advance the price, terms and conditions and quality standards with those interested in bidding. To maximise the efficiency of the marketplace, the work might be divided into value ranges, thus allowing each bidder to pitch for one or more of the value bands. This allows the smaller service provider to compete with the larger consultancies on lower value projects without the need to pitch for the bigger projects, where the likelihood of success (based on experience) would be limited. Typical question formats are shown in Figure 1.1.

A framework contract will not necessarily guarantee you the work, it simply means that you have been put on a shortlist and may still have to bid for each project as it comes up. Some frameworks are structured in such a way that the projects are given out in rotation to those on the list, so as not to commit too much work to one supplier and risk overloading them. This method rewards all those who made it through to the shortlist.

Fee proposal			
Select which of the following project values you wish to be considered for and enter your fee percentage			
Project value	£100k–£500k	£500k–£1m	£1m–£1.5m
Proposed fee			

Relevant experience
Select which of the project values you wish to be considered for and describe your experience, in the past *three* years, of providing services or works similar to those being sought under this contract. A minimum of *three* projects to be detailed for each value band selected. As a minimum requirement, the following should be provided for each project:
• name of client • brief description of project • start/end dates • contract value (£)

FIGURE 1.1: Typical questions within a framework bid document

The benefits of a framework agreement are that it:

- offers the client reduced fee values due to the promise of a given volume of work
- gives the consultants the opportunity of regular work
- allows the consultants to maintain a dedicated team that will get to know how the client operates and their required procedures. This also benefits the client in that there is experience and knowledge transfer from one project to the next, so projects should run more smoothly and efficiently.

Therefore, when bidding for a framework contract, you should bear in mind:

- not to overcommit by bidding for too many categories if your resources are stretched
- only to target those value bands where you have a good chance of winning, as a weak submission in one area may reduce the potential client's overall perception of your abilities
- if possible, being more competitive on fees, given the fact there may be regular work on several projects over a number of years.

Ways to make a bid

Bidding as part of a team (collaborative working)

Clients increasingly want a single point of contact when dealing with their consultant's team. Some bidding opportunities will stipulate that the client is looking for a full team with one member acting as a key contact to coordinate or manage the other team members.

When forming a team to bid for a project, consider what the client may be looking for. The client, or their advisers, may be evaluating your past experience of working together on similar projects, as well as the adequacy of your current resources to undertake the proposed project. Therefore, if you find yourself in this situation, make sure you are joining a team which has winning potential. There is no point in including another consultancy in your team which does not meet the client's selection criteria. Equally, if you are invited to join a team and you believe that your firm does not meet the criteria, then it is best to decline and wait for a more appropriate opportunity.

On some very small projects, the client may not be particularly concerned about the other professionals that you involve, in which case there may be other commercial factors that determine your selection. If you are introducing new firms to your client, see if they will reciprocate and introduce you to their clients.

One word of caution here (and you may need to speak to your insurers): make sure that you don't take on responsibility for other consultants' design or technical input. If possible, each firm should have a separate contract with the client, even though one firm becomes the key interface with the client.

Bidding as a subcontractor (design and build)

Many of the larger contractors offer a design and build service. This involves undertaking to design the building using either their own in-house designers or a team they have selected specifically for the project. Once the design is finalised, they proceed to build the project. This service has many advantages for the client, offering:

- an all-inclusive price, which is often fixed at the outset of the project
- a single point of contact and one line of responsibility for the design and construction
- reduced risk for the client.

The main disadvantages for the client tend to be the lack of influence over the choice of consultant and insufficient time to develop the designs. However, these drawbacks can be overcome by using novation. Novation involves the client picking a design team to take the brief and develop the designs up to a certain stage – either to an outline stage (RIBA Stage C) with outline planning consent, or to a more detailed stage (RIBA Stage D) with, perhaps, full planning approval.

At this stage, the scheme forms part of the tender process and the design team is novated to the successful contractor, becoming part of the contractor's team. Sometimes a quantity surveyor may be retained by the client to advise on costs and contract administration. Alternatively, the design team may stay with the client and monitor the contractor's design team's design development. The benefit of not having the design team novated is that the contractor's team may come up with innovative solutions that may reduce costs, save time and increase buildability.

Therefore, in a design and build situation there is scope to bid to the client or, if there is no novation, to bid to the contractor as a subcontractor. When considering bidding for work to a contractor on a subcontractor basis, take into account the following questions:

- Does the contractor have a good success rate?
- How many are being asked to tender? (That is, how many consultants are bidding to the contractor and, in turn, how many contractors are bidding to the client?)
- Who are the competitors and are they more likely to win?
- Does the contractor have a good relationship with the client?
- What input would be required at the tender stage?

Bearing in mind the above, you should take a commercial view on the likely success of the tender. Unfortunately, in this situation you probably do not have direct contact with the contractor's client and it may be difficult to obtain all the information you need to make a well-informed decision.

Some consultants will feel that they are better suited to work for, and remain with, the client in a design and build project. Alternatively, some consultants have the skill sets to help contractors tender for these design and build opportunities. Your choice of which of these two roles to bid for will determine which of your skills you emphasise in the bid document.

When bidding to the client	Emphasise your strengths in the following areas:
	• brief taking
	• ability to liaise with stakeholders and keep them on side
	• good concept design
	• good at securing planning permission, especially on difficult sites, if applicable (such as conservation areas)
	• ability to work efficiently with the contractor's design team
	• good at monitoring the design development and making sure that the key design principles are maintained.

When bidding to the contractor	Emphasise the following strengths:
	• the ability to quickly evaluate a design concept and work to strict tender deadlines
	• the ability to innovate – being able to modify the design concept (within the original design team's parameters) to deliver solutions that are more economical and quicker to build
	• the ability to provide key detailed information quickly so that the contractor can obtain competitive prices from suppliers and subcontractors
	• having the relevant skills and experience, which will be attractive to the client's evaluation team when they are considering the tender documents.

In a high proportion of design and build projects, the design team is novated to the successful contractor. In these situations, the consultants may have to adapt to the needs of their new client. A successful project may lead to repeat work, either from the original client or from the contractor, on future design and build opportunities.

E-procurement and e-auctions

E-procurement

Electronic purchasing techniques are becoming more prevalent, especially where there are strict rules governing word or character limits for answers to questions. In such cases, access to an e-procurement website is provided using secure, password-protected registration procedures.

Those bidding will then either type in their response to specific questions or upload specific documents, such as company accounts and certificates. Questions which have a word or character limit may prevent the inclusion of extra text. After the deadline has passed, further access to the site may be denied.

Be aware that if you wait until the last moment to send your electronic bid there is a risk that:

• your internet connection may go down
• with everybody submitting at the last minute, the client's server may be slow
• a problem may arise in sending one of the files or electronic attachments
• some files may prove to be too big to send and you may need to consider changing the electronic format.

More frequently, clients may ask for both a hard copy and an electronic version to allow them to print further copies if they need to. When submitting an electronic copy, consider how your submission will appear if printed in black and white rather than in colour.

E-auctions

E-auctions are now being used for service contracts where previously they were only used for purchasing goods. Leading up to the e-auction, the consultant will prepare and submit the tender documents in the usual way. The price submitted will, however, be seen purely as an opening indicative offer. After the client has evaluated the submissions, those shortlisted will be invited to the e-auction.

Bidders will be asked to log onto the web-based auction and will be required to make their first anonymous bid. As the e-auction proceeds, the bidders can make further bids, reducing the price with each subsequent bid. The bidders will see their competitors' anonymous bids. The auction ends when the lowest bid is made.

In some e-auctions, the lowest price may not necessarily win. Knowing what your lowest bid was, the client can consider that alongside your technical submission and may apply a weighting to arrive at the overall winner.

Bidding through procurement agencies

The whole bid process can be time consuming for the client, especially if they have a large portfolio of work to place. Many public sector clients now tend to use third party organisations to deal with the pre-qualification stage. The client will agree the selection criteria and the third party procurement agency will handle the shortlisting stage. Once shortlisted in this accreditation stage, the consultant can pre-qualify for many more projects without the need to complete a fresh pre-qualification for each one.

Sometimes, one public sector client will create their own accreditation stage and give other public sector clients access to the consultants who have pre-qualified against pre-agreed criteria. This can reduce the costs for those bidding, as well as the client's procurement costs.

▶ SUMMARY CHECKLIST

- Do you have all, or most, of the attributes to successfully create winning bids?
- Even in negotiated opportunities, submit good proposal documentation so as not to give the client a reason to seek alternative proposals
- Public sector projects follow set procedures, but these should not deter the smaller firms
- Smaller firms may wish to target low-value projects within the public sector, as these have simpler procedures
- Framework contracts can offer potential workload over a longer period on several projects. To increase chances of success, only pursue the project value bands that match your experience and capability
- If you are considering joining other consultants to form a team to pitch to a client, be very selective. Don't include weak team members that may not have the relevant experience or resources and may jeopardise your chances of winning the project
- Be equally selective in your choice of contractor when considering design and build opportunities. Consider their success rates and the relationship they have with the potential client
- If submitting bids electronically, leave yourself sufficient time to send the files, especially if they are large. Consider also how your submission will look if printed out by the client in black and white rather than in colour
- Consider the benefits of pre-qualification through a procurement agency, which could give you access to many clients

CHAPTER 2
What to establish before tender or pre-qualification release

The need for background information

To improve your chances of preparing a successful bid, you should know as much as possible about the client. That means doing some research before the opportunity to submit a bid arises. The level of research will depend on your available resources and current commitments. Once several firms have been invited to submit proposals, there is usually limited time and restricted access to the client. So undertake as much preparatory work as possible – it might make the difference between success and failure in your bid.

Questions can usually still be asked during the bid stage, but the disadvantage is that they have to be submitted in writing and the answers are circulated to all those bidding. If you want to have a competitive advantage over your competitors, find out as much as possible about the project and the client before the formal bidding process starts.

Things to know before the documentation is received

Listed below are 25 aspects of a project that you should know about before the bid process officially starts. Smaller firms with limited resources might find it difficult to devote sufficient time to uncovering all this information and may need to be selective. Larger firms, however, might have a client capture or project capture process in place, especially when chasing very large projects.

The project

1 What is the scope of the project?
If the project involves several different functional elements, then it is important to know what these are before the bid is released to the marketplace. Knowing as much as possible about the project in advance can help you to take appropriate steps to ensure that you are fully prepared to make a successful bid.

2 Are there any gaps in your ability to fulfil the requirements?
The client may have some particular requirements with respect to your capabilities. You may have to demonstrate particular experience in similar projects, of similar value and, possibly,

in a certain geographical area. If you are unable to satisfy these minimum requirements you may have reason to doubt the probability of success and decide not to bid.

3 Are you able to fill any gaps in capabilities through association with others?
If you become aware of any gaps in your capabilities sufficiently early in the process, there may be an opportunity to address them. By associating with another firm you may be able to offer the specific experience, resources and skills to fit the contract requirements.

4 Which previous projects will you use to establish your credibility?
To improve your chances of preparing a winning bid you will need to demonstrate that you have the relevant experience and capability. There is no better way to do so than by referring to recently completed buildings similar to the one being considered. Having sufficient advance notice of the project, and any particular requirements, will allow you to prepare project profiles or case studies to demonstrate your ability.

Make these project profiles or case studies specific to the opportunity being pursued. If, from your research, you find there are, say, three key issues that will determine the selection of the consultant, then bring these points out in the project case study and feature them in the appropriate order of priority. For instance, if the client is looking for a consultant who can handle a multi-floor office refurbishment while some areas of the building remain in occupation, then you should highlight that aspect of your abilities in the reference projects you select to showcase.

5 Do you have the relevant third party endorsements to provide credibility?
Clients like, and are reassured by, third party endorsements. If you are able to obtain good, relevant client endorsements then this will give your bid more credibility. Again, knowing about particular aspects of the project in advance will give you sufficient time to obtain the relevant client quotes.

Wherever possible, make the endorsements relevant to the project being targeted. Perhaps ask your clients to highlight certain aspects of your service. If the project for which you are bidding requires the refurbishment of a Grade II listed building, then ask a past client to comment on how successful you were in refurbishing their Grade II listed building. This commentary might feature how well you managed the planning approval stage, your devotion to historical detail or other key aspects of dealing with listed building projects.

6 Who are the internal and external experts who may need to be involved in preparing the proposal?
With sufficient advance notice of the bid, and detail about the proposed project, you will be able to earmark the relevant internal resources to create the bid. There may also be an

element of the project that will require external input. This could be in preparing graphics, taking professional photographs of reference projects or ensuring that key individuals are available to write relevant sections of the bid.

There may be a need to call in some external experts to give you a competitive edge – perhaps industry experts who will be available to help the client during the briefing stage or an external consultant with a niche skill set.

The project programme

7   What is driving the client's procurement programme?

Some projects may have extremely tight programmes and it is useful to know what is driving these deadlines. Sometimes, however, the client wishes a project to be designed and built quickly but might not realise that this may have cost implications. Some clients may relax the programme if there is a demonstrable cost benefit.

Where a tight programme is unavoidable, then being aware of this before the bid opportunity is released may allow you to do some preparatory work. This preparatory work could give the client the impression that you would be able to start the process more quickly than your competitors, thereby giving you a distinct advantage. You may also be able to prepare some advice on various procurement methods that could lead to an earlier completion date. The more proactive you are seen to be, the better your chances of winning the bid.

You might give some thought to certain design elements of the project being able to use off-site construction, enabling them to be brought to site and installed at the appropriate stage in the project's completion. Alternatively, there may be an opportunity to take elements of the project with long lead-in times off the critical path, thereby reducing the overall programme. Consideration of such innovative options may impress the client when evaluating your proposal.

8   What are the key milestone events within the client's procurement programme?

Many projects have important milestone events that drive the procurement programme. Perhaps there is a need to complete elements of the building within a certain time so that the client can qualify for a government grant. Alternatively, some buildings projects are driven by their use. Education projects may have to be ready for the new intake of students. Other projects may have funding available only within a certain financial year.

Some of the reasons for milestone events may not be obvious in the bid documents. The more you know in advance, the more fully you will be able to address these issues during the bid preparation stage, which will help to differentiate you from your competitors.

9 When will the tender or pre-qualification documentation be released?

Knowing when the bid documentation will be released will enable you to keep a close eye on its progress. Knowing when to expect the documents may give you the opportunity to:

- arrange a meeting with the client before the documentation is released in order to obtain more detail about the project, thus giving you an advantage over your competitors
- give a presentation to the client team, especially if you don't know whether you have made the shortlist
- keep your bid team informed of any delays in bid document release or postponement of the project.

Some public sector projects might require you to formally express an interest in a project by having to reply within a certain time limit to an official notice in the *Official Journal of the European Union* (*OJEU*).

10 How much time will there be to prepare the proposal?

Knowing how much time there will be to prepare the bid proposal will help you to manage your internal resources. This is particularly important during busy times, especially holiday periods.

Sometimes, if there is already an incumbent consultant on board, who will also be competing for the project, only a short time may be allocated to preparing the documentation, which may be a deliberate strategy to give the incumbent team an advantage.

Knowing the schedule in advance may give you the opportunity to lobby the client for additional time. This might be more acceptable for the client to agree before the documents are released.

Approach to procurement

11 What is the client's approach to procurement?

It would be advantageous to know if the client has a preferred approach to procurement. This may be driven by:

- level of risk that is acceptable
- the need to have a firm fixed price
- the desire to have a single point of responsibility (as in the design and build approach)
- a need to complete as fast as possible
- the ability to select consultants separately from the selection of the building contractor.

Once you know what is driving the procurement strategy, you will be able to write your bid accordingly. Do not attempt to change the client's approach. If you believe there is a better way to undertake the project, which has client benefits rather than being merely your preference, then by all means show this as an alternative. You will then be able to set out the benefits that the alternative has for the client over the original procurement method. If you only put forward the alternative, then the client will not know how your proposal compares with the original approach and may doubt your motives.

If the client is silent on the approach to procurement then consider whether you need to address it. If certain outcomes are required, such as a single point of responsibility, then you may feel the need to put forward the design and build approach (with or without your novation for continued involvement). Always consider how the client will view your proposals and always spell out the advantages and benefits to the client.

12   Is the client assisted by external advisers or consultants?

It may be necessary to adopt a different approach to your bid if you are aware that the client is being assisted by external advisers or consultants. Once you become aware that these advisers or consultants exist, you must establish whether:

- they are to play a role after your appointment – if so, what will their role be?
- they have strong links with any of your competitors who might also be putting forward a bid – if so, do you consider that the selection has already been made and the client is just going through the process of obtaining additional bids?
- these external advisers and consultants have a preferred way of working that may influence the selection – if so, then address these points and preferences in your bid.

Competitors

13   Do you know who your competitors will be?

It is very useful to know if you will be in a competitive environment or if certain competitors are already being considered. Try to establish:

- whether there is already an incumbent competitor – if so, consider why the client might be considering others. Is it to test the market on price in an attempt to reduce the incumbent's bid?
- whether your competitors have a better relationship with the client?
- if you can detect any bias towards your competitors?

If you are not aware of any competitors and you suspect that you are currently the only firm being considered, it would be best not to ask about competitors as this might prompt the client to consider others. This is particular relevant in smaller projects where clients are more likely to negotiate with a single consultancy and not seek alternative bids.

Selection process and evaluation criteria

14   Is there a formal selection process and evaluation criteria? If so, what are they?
Some bid documents will declare the evaluation method. The most common is a combination of scores for technical competence (determined by how well you answered the questions), cost (your fee) and possibly how your team performed at a presentation.

There might be a three-stage process where the first stage is based purely on your suitability and how you have addressed the technical questions (the quality of your bid submission), followed by a presentation and then negotiation of fees with the preferred consultant. An example of award criteria is shown in Figure 2.1.

Knowing how the bid is going to be marked is very valuable information. In the example shown in Figure 2.1, it is clear that the client places a high value on quality, service and technical ability. So, if you are well-established and can demonstrate those qualities, this would be the ideal project to pursue. Alternatively, if your quality, service and technical ability are not as good as your competitor's, then perhaps your time would be better spent pursuing those contracts where the value for money rating is much higher. This type of contract would be ideal if you have low overheads and believe you can deliver the right level of quality, service and technical ability at a lower cost than your competitors. Notice the need for financial stability highlighted in Figure 2.1. If you have a poor set of accounts then perhaps this contract is not for you.

Individual questions will probably have marks allocated to them. If you know the scoring matrix, then your submission should reflect this. Your answer for a question where the answer is only allocated five marks will be shorter than an answer attracting a score of 25 marks, especially if there is a page or word limit.

However, no matter what score the question attracts, give your best possible answer. It might just be that only a few marks will separate you from your competitors.

Award criteria	
The award of the contract will be made based on the most economically advantageous tender in terms of the following criteria:	
Value for money	20%
Quality, service and technical ability	80%
Financial stability	Requirement

FIGURE 2.1: Example of award criteria

15   If there is no declared selection procedure, what are the client's unwritten selection and evaluation criteria?

Not all bid documentation comes with an indication of the selection criteria. Therefore, before the bid documents are released, meet with the client, or their retained advisers, to establish how they will select the consultants.

If the client has retained advisers there will almost certainly be some sort of selection criteria, although they might not be prepared to disclose it. If no evaluation criteria are apparent, when speaking with the client try to establish their preferences. Perhaps even prepare your own selection criteria to table at the meeting so that at least you can establish levels of priority. This knowledge will help you to reflect the client's levels of priority in your bid submission. Also, by tabling your own criteria you might be able to influence the client to take on board some of your suggestions. This can be particularly useful if it gives you an advantage. For example, you may be local to the project and be aware that your main competitors are not. You might be able to persuade the client to consider the various benefits of having someone with local knowledge.

16   How are you positioned in terms of the evaluation criteria?

Do an analysis of the evaluation criteria and take a realistic view of your potential to win. If you are lacking in relevant experience and that is the key element in the evaluation, then you need to question whether you should waste time and money submitting a bid.

You should have a 'bid or no bid' review at this stage. Also, consider if your best team is available to undertake the project.

17   Are your competitors better positioned in terms of the evaluation criteria?

As part of your 'bid or no bid' review, consider how you are positioned with regard to your competitors. Do the evaluation criteria and scoring matrix favour you or your competitors?

It would be beneficial to score yourself and your competitors according to what you know about the client and their advisers, bearing in mind any known preferences or incumbent competitors. Taking a realistic view at this stage will help to determine your probability of success.

If you don't know who your competitors are, then score yourself against an imaginary competitor who might also be pitching for the project.

18   Are you able to influence the client's evaluation criteria by bringing some additional added value?

The key to scoring high marks, and thus being successful in your bid, is to answer fully all the questions to the best of your ability. But to differentiate yourself and increase your chances of success, always try to include additional, but relevant, information.

This additional information should demonstrate some sort of added value or additional benefits to the client. For example, the bid might ask you to list all your relevant experience in the same sector. Having answered this, you may go on to say that you also have wide experience of the same building type but in different sectors. For example, you may be pitching for a university laboratory and research centre. The fact that you have additional experience in designing laboratories for the pharmaceutical industry will also be relevant, as long as you explain the benefits. In this example you could suggest that your knowledge acquired in working for the pharmaceutical sector would bring current thinking and best practice to the design. Always be on the lookout for ways to demonstrate your transferable skills and experience to the benefit of the client.

Financial – how is the project funded?

19   Is funding in place?

Most projects are driven by funding. If no funding is in place then the project is unlikely to proceed. Consider the following points:

- The client might be a building contractor and is asking you to do work up front on a 'no job, no fee' basis.
- The project might be speculative and would require some grant funding from a government body.
- The project might not be able to attract funding unless a certain level of development is achieved and this might be dependent on planning approvals.
- Funding may only be available within a certain time period. The start and end dates of the project may determine funding availability.

You may consider the opportunity to be involved with a particular project, even though it might not proceed, to be a worthwhile objective. There might even be a limited fee available for initial work.

Once you have decided that it is worth bidding, use the financial information to your advantage. Perhaps feature your experience in preparing designs that are capable of attracting grant funding, or your ability to have the building completed within the relevant time periods to be eligible for funding.

Always look at what is driving the project and, where appropriate, show off your skill and experience to secure the project for your team.

20   What is the estimated value of the project?

The value of the project might have a bearing on your chances of success:

- The project might be too big – if the value is several times greater than your biggest previous project, the client and their advisers might consider it too risky to place the work with you. This would be particularly true if your competitors have experience of buildings of similar value to that under consideration.

- The project might be too small – your firm might be geared up to handle medium to large buildings and your fees, due to overheads, might reflect this. If you suddenly decide to pitch for work much smaller in scale than you normally undertake, your fees might be too high. Also, smaller projects might attract different competitors who would be able to work at reduced fee levels.
- Larger projects may require more professional indemnity insurance cover with additional premiums – consider whether this will be a one-off large project or if it will be a business objective to pursue bigger schemes in the future.

21   Is it possible to vary the scope to reduce the budget?

As part of your bid you might be able to offer suggestions on how the project could be reduced in cost and still retain its function. This will be particularly relevant if you are pitching in a design and build situation with the contractor as your direct client. Often, design and build bids come with a scheme, which will need to be worked up.

If you are able to introduce some innovative ideas and offer some alternatives, then you might be able to make your proposal more attractive.

Key contacts

22   Have you identified the key decision makers, influencers, stakeholders and external advisers?

Very early on in your dealings with the client you should find out who all the relevant people are. Few, perhaps only one person, will be able to make the final decision. However, there may be others who may be able to influence that decision. There will also be some people who will be involved in the process, perhaps just at the briefing stage, whom it would be good to have on side.

During the relationship-building stage it is important to find out the aspects of the project in which each relevant group or individual has an interest. Once you are able to identify their interests or concerns, you have an opportunity to address these points in your bid and, in particular, at any follow-up presentation.

Once you have identified each person, build up a person profile. You may be able to ask for their curriculum vitae (CV) or career details. This information may be available on the internet (on sites such as LinkedIn). If the client is a company that produces an annual report, a given individual might contribute to that report, especially if they are the managing director or another key director or chairman. An annual report will often also contain potted biographies of directors and key senior managers. Take the time before

Key individuals within client organisation				
Potential client: AB & C Industries				
Proposed project: new offices and production facility				
Individual involvement	Name	Job title	Relationship: Hot (H) Warm (W) Cold (C)	Comments
Sign off	Brian Jones	Managing Director	C	Only met once so not sure he knows our capability. His key concern is for the building to reflect the quality of their products (good quality and innovative). Need to meet again if possible before bidding to improve the relationship and raise his awareness of our experience
Technical evaluation and selection	Henry James	Procurement Manager	H	Good relationship. He is very keen on sustainability and reduction of running costs. Wants to know pay-back periods for any enhanced specification. He has visited our Bolton project and was very interested in heat pumps and heat recovery. Has advised that he needs to obtain three bids
End users	Jill Farmer	Facilities Manager	W	Very interested in workstation design that offers hot desking possibilities for the sales team
	Stuart Cuthbert	Works Manager	W	Mentioned that he wants clean, smooth surfaces in production facility to make cleaning easier
Influencer	Dan King	Former Managing Director, now retired	C	Although retired, has been brought back for one day per week to help with drafting the brief. He will probably have an influence on the selection of consultants

FIGURE 2.2: Example of client record showing key interests of those involved within the client organisation

the bid documents are issued to find out as much as you can about these individuals and discover what you could say in the bid documents that would favour your selection.

23   How good are your relationships with the key decision makers and influencers?
Take some time to evaluate your relationship with the client. This may influence your 'bid or no bid' decision. Record information in your client relationship management (CRM) package
There are many off-the-shelf CRM packages that enable you to record key information about your client and ongoing relationship development. Alternatively, create your own record to suit your specific needs. The type of information that would be useful to record is shown in Figure 2.2, in which the following can be seen:

- There are four levels of individual involvement within the client organisation. These being sign off, technical evaluation and selection, end users and influencers. Each will have a contribution to make in the final designs and may be involved in the selection process.
- The comments section clearly shows the key issues that have been uncovered so far. It would therefore be wise to cover these points in the bid documentation and demonstrate, with project profiles or client endorsements, the experience and capability available within the consultancy to address these issues.
- A good relationship has been established with Henry James. There is a need to improve the relationship with Mary Jones (managing director) and the former managing director, Dan King, who may be a key influencer in the selection process.

From Figure 2.2 it can be seen how useful it is to record information about your potential clients. Although not shown in the example, it may also be useful to record their outside interests. For example, if you find out that the key decision-making person plays team sports, then the language of your bid might reflect the team ethos and winning strategies. Using language that your clients can latch on to is a valuable ingredient in your bid-drafting process.

Given that there may be several people who are either decision makers or key influencers, reflect all their individual characters in the bid. For example, the managing director might be focusing more on the big picture and brand value, the financial director on cost certainty and value for money and the operations director on completing on time and according to programme. This will give you an opportunity to use slightly different language in each section. Obviously, each section will need to be similar in style and format but language could tend to reflect the targeted readership of a given section.

24   Are there opportunities to enhance the relationships prior to the
      documentation being issued?
Having identified who the key decision makers and influencers are, try to enhance the relationships prior to the bid process. This can be achieved in the following ways:

- Request an opportunity to meet and get to know more about the project. If the client refuses, or says the approach is premature, then obtain permission to keep in touch so that you are able to track developments. If this is again refused, then you should seriously question your chances of success.
- Once you know more about the project and the client, contact them and request an opportunity to present your capabilities, either in a formal or an informal presentation.
- If you have identified particular projects that you have undertaken which might be relevant to the proposed project, try to organise a client visit to these projects. During the visit try to arrange for your past client to meet the potential client so that they can endorse your capability and suitability. Client endorsements are very influential.
- Send the potential client newsletters, project profiles and other relevant literature that raises your profile. Be careful not to overdo it and be selective in what you communicate. If you send information which is not relevant, it will dilute the message you are trying to convey. For example, if you are hoping to bid for an office project do not send information about a school project unless there is a very relevant aspect that will be of interest to the client.

25   What are the lines of communication?

During your interaction with the client, take care to establish the correct lines of communication. If you have developed a rapport with someone in the client organisation, do not then communicate with others without the approval of the first contact. You might find out that your initial contact has to report upwards internally and you may be tempted to start communicating directly with the more senior person. Handle the situation carefully. The last thing you want to do is to alienate your original contact.

If necessary, create a chart of the client organisation and determine who reports to whom and their individual responsibilities.

▶ **SUMMARY CHECKLIST**

◆ Carry out research before the tender or pre-qualification documentation is released, specifically to do with:
  - project scope and how it impacts on your approach to the bid
  - the project programme
  - the approach to procurement
  - selection and evaluation criteria
  - project funding
  - key contacts and relationships
  - competitors

CHAPTER 3
Credibility, capability, compatibility and reliability (the 3Cs + R test)

The 3Cs + R test

When preparing a bid, it is always important to establish the purpose of the questions that are being asked. Ask yourself what the client is trying to find out. Most questions will require you to prove one of the following:

- Credibility (convincing the client that they can believe your claims).
- Capability (convincing the client that you have the experience and adequate resources to undertake the assignment).
- Compatibility (convincing the client that they can work with you and that there is a cultural fit).
- Reliability (convincing the client that you will do what you claim you can do).

Credibility and capability are relatively easy to address. You should be able to prove that you have the appropriate level of experience and that you currently have sufficient resources to undertake the project. The skill lies in really showing off your abilities and making yourself stand out from the competitors.

Compatibility and reliability will take more effort to address and sometimes your qualities in these respects might be examined indirectly rather than directly questioned. So, when preparing your documentation, check that you are able to demonstrate both of these qualities.

When evaluating your submission, the client can make a rational evaluation of your capability, credibility and reliability. This evaluation can be based on examination of your references, endorsements, accreditation, experience and qualifications of your proposed team. Compatibility, however, requires a non-rational evaluation. The client will have to rely on 'gut instinct' in determining whether they and their team will be able to work with you and your team.

Credibility

Clients will want to be reassured that they can believe all the claims that you make. To help with this aspect of the bid you should deliver your message with confidence and enthusiasm. Use positive language and refrain from using weak words (see Figure 3.1).

Avoid	Why to avoid and possible alternatives
• We intend to • We will try to • We will attempt to • We hope to • We can	The client is not concerned with what you will attempt or try to do but what you *will* do, so say: *"We will do"*
• Your prestigious project	Only use if it really *is* a prestigious project. This phrase is not suitable for a small building extension
• We are dedicated to • We are committed to	Your dedication and commitment is worthless if you don't deliver. Again, say: *"We will do"* or *"We are going to"*
• We understand • We believe • We think	This is weak. Turn your statement around to sound more positive and add a benefit. So rather than: *"We understand you require zero defects at completion"* say: *"We will monitor the construction works and liaise with the contractor so at the time of handover there will be zero defects thereby causing no disruption once the building is occupied."* Notice in this phrase there is not only a statement (feature) but also the benefit (no disruption once occupied)
• We are the best • We are leading edge • We are pioneering	Don't use. If you want to make the same point then substantiate it by adding a client benefit. So say something like: *"We have recently received a regional design award. The award-winning team will be available for this project, delivering the very best architectural design."*

FIGURE 3.1: Words or phrases to avoid

Another useful tool when writing bids is the use of a presupposition. A presupposition involves using words that give the impression that an idea or experience is presumed without actually saying so. For example:

- 'Have you now started to win work?'
  This presupposes that you have been losing work.

Examples of some phrases that you could introduce in your proposals are:

- 'This is one of the cost-saving elements of our proposal.'
  This assumes that there is more than one cost-saving element.

- 'Another feature that will deliver distinct benefits is ...'
  This assumes that there are other features giving distinct benefits.

- 'Looking at your brief I am sure this will be one of the advantages that will really interest you.'
  This assumes that there are several advantages.

To enhance your credibility, have facts and figures at hand to back up your statements.

Rather than saying, 'We are very experienced in designing schools', say something like:

- 'In the past five years we have designed 15 schools, providing facilities for over 6,000 pupils with a total contract value of £75 million.'

In this example, if the project you are bidding for is a school extension to provide a facility for performing arts, then you might wish to say something like:

- 'In the past five years we have been involved in extending six schools, providing new additional accommodation. Three of these projects incorporated new performing arts facilities. In all cases, the schools continued to function without disruption during construction. In the same period, we were also involved with 15 new schools, providing facilities for 6,000 additional pupils. Five of these schools also had performing arts facilities. Therefore, our total school experience in the past five years includes 21 schools (eight with new performing arts facilities) with a total contract value of £93 million.'

This modified answer has the advantage of:

- placing the most relevant experience first (extending a facility to include performing arts accommodation)
- following up with additional relevant experience, albeit in slightly different circumstances (total of new schools with performing arts facilities)
- including some benefits (no disruption to existing schools during the extension works)
- giving an indication of the total school experience (21 schools with a total contract value of £93 million).

This would also be backed up with several of the most relevant project profiles or case studies.

To build up your credibility you may add additional information that is relevant and might set you apart from competitors. For instance, in the performing arts example above there may be a need for specialist acoustic advice to enhance the acoustics in the auditorium area. This might not have been identified or specified by the client and, by raising the point and offering this specialist additional service within your bid, you may set yourself apart from the competition.

Capability

This is probably the easiest part to prove and is often the area on which most clients, or their advisers, focus. At the very least, you will need to demonstrate the following three aspects:

Track record
You will have to show that you have undertaken several assignments that are relevant and similar to the project for which you are bidding. Obviously, feature the projects that are the closest match and include other projects that have relevant transferable experience which would be beneficial to the client.

Include project sheets, case studies, client references and endorsements. Always, if time permits, rewrite the project sheets and case studies to bring out the relevant information. Also, sequence the information in the appropriate order of priority to reflect the client's needs.

If you do not have exactly the experience being sought, then try to accentuate the following aspects:

- Select elements of your past projects that may have relevant or similar features or use. For example, a sporting facility for a school may be seen as a matching experience for a public or university sporting facility.

- Show that you have certain skills that are transferable and which would be appropriate and beneficial to the proposed project. If the project is a refurbishment involving many phases, during which some parts will remain in occupation, then a similar project showing your ability to manage a refurbishment while the client is in occupation may make you stand out from the competitors. This might still be of interest to the client even if the building type is not exactly the same.

- If the project is much bigger than any of your previous projects then, if applicable, show that the combined value of projects going through your office at any given time exceeds that of the project being considered. Then perhaps you could argue that managing one larger project is easier than managing, say, two smaller ones which together exceed the value of the bigger one.

- If the client perceives that the project is too big for you to handle, then take time to submit a fully worked out resource schedule. This will identify your team members and show their availability at the appropriate times to fulfil their role in the project. You will need to show their other commitments to give credibility to your schedule. Always demonstrate, if possible, that you even have spare capacity should projects be delayed or revisions have to be accommodated.

Technical ability and insight into client's business and sector	The client will take comfort from knowing that you have relevant sector and building-type experience. Clients do not want to educate their consultants. You will need to show that you not only have that specific knowledge but also that it is up to date and perhaps that you are able to bring added value to the project with the latest thinking and innovation.
Application	It is one thing to have the track record and technical ability, but within your bid you will also have to demonstrate how you can adapt to suit the specific client's needs. By using examples from your other projects, show how your skill and experience resulted in benefits to the clients.

Compatibility

Most of your competitors will be homing in on the rational criteria, as these are the easiest to demonstrate through project profiles and client endorsements. Because of the effort required, many consultants do not tackle the compatibility angle. This is why clients tend to be more comfortable working with consultants that they have worked with before.

If you have not worked with the client before, it is vital that you try to build up your compatibility credentials during the pre-bid and bidding stages. Some of your competitors will try to give the client a sense of how well they will be able to work together. The smarter professional will seek to give the potential client an insight into how this might operate. This can be achieved by engaging with the client while you are shaping your service delivery within your bid documentation. You should let the client sample your thinking processes and working methods. Familiarity can be built up through an interactive process, so it is important to have laid the foundations of the relationship before the bid documents are issued. This can be achieved by the following actions:

- Defining the client's needs whenever possible – ask the client for more detail and clarification, but don't make a nuisance of yourself.

- Defining the problems – try to get the client to elaborate on the thinking behind the needs. What is to be solved and who are the stakeholders that need to be satisfied?
- Exploring the implications of the problem solving – will other issues arise that will need to be addressed?

By having this two-way dialogue with the client you will be able to uncover how the client thinks and evaluates their own needs. You will also, along the way, build up a rapport which may also extend to other decision makers, influencers and stakeholders. This will be a great advantage during the bid evaluation period. Your bid is more likely to receive a favourable evaluation if you are known to the client and have been seen to take an active and thorough interest in the project leading up to the bid.

Depending on the timing and circumstances leading up to the bid process, you may be able to further your compatibility rating with the client by the following means:

- Inviting them to workshops or seminars that will build up your credibility as well as compatibility. These might also include seminars delivered by leading experts in a particular field which are not being organised by you. For example, if your client is in the education sector there might be an educational conference with a speaker talking about how the design of buildings can help to reduce bullying in schools. This approach might work particularly well with public sector clients. They might find it difficult to accept hospitality to, say, sporting events, but could attend a function which is of direct relevance to the project or their work.
- Inviting them to visit one of your projects and meet one of your satisfied clients. There is nothing better than walking around a project and discussing the client's issues; much invaluable information can be gained from such a visit.

Building on what you learn during this interaction with the client, you will be able to include within the bid submission:

- your process or methodology, which would reflect how the client wants to run the project
- the key issues that may not be highlighted in the bid documentation. Furthermore your client interaction may also give you an indication of the order of priority of the key issues, which can then be reflected in your submission
- the client's language, idiom or jargon.

It is not always possible to meet the client before the bid documents are received. In this instance, other research needs to be undertaken to give you an insight into the client's organisation and gain information that you can incorporate into your bid. You can do this by researching the following:

Annual directors' report	The key directors of larger client organisations in the private sector will issue an annual report. Elements of the report that may be of particular interest will be the statements about the future growth of the business, which may provide an insight into the need for additional facilities. Also, make a note of any mission, purpose and value statements and examine their corporate responsibility statement.
Website	There may be valuable information on the client's website, which may give you a feel for their approach. Are they driven by money and profit? Are they concerned about sustainability and social responsibility? Are they process and results driven? All these aspects may help you to select the tone and language in your bid documentation. Also, take a look at the news or media section on the website as this will show how the client wants to be perceived within the community.
Articles	Some of the larger organisations will have articles written about them or their key individuals. These articles might contain information that you can use.

As part of the selection process, the bid documents may ask about your approach to working within a team. This may be of particular interest within a framework contract where the client wants to be reassured that the consultants can work together and share relevant experience. The client will look for compatibility within the teams as well as an ethos of sharing good practice and innovative ideas. A typical question found in bid documents is shown in Figure 3.2.

Collaborative working
Using examples from past projects, explain how good practice developed in one project has been successfully rolled out to another region or team. In particular, demonstrate how innovation and sharing new ideas with other teams has taken place

FIGURE 3.2: A typical question within a bid document regarding collaborative working

The question in Figure 3.2 is looking for evidence that you have achieved the following:

- passed on good practice from one project to another where you have been involved in a series of projects for a client – this is especially important if several projects are running together using different teams
- been involved in a framework contract involving your competitors, have a process in place to record best practice and demonstrate that you have, in the past, cooperated

with your competitors for the benefit of an overall programme of work. This might involve 'lessons learned' workshops, monthly meetings with other consultants to share ideas and feedback on projects or a shared website to record information that may be of benefit to other project teams

- demonstrated the ability to be innovative and come up with new ideas that deliver client benefits.

The whole question of compatibility also applies to the team members. This is why clients like to have a team of professionals who have worked successfully together before on similar projects.

Reliability

The other key element that clients will look for is reliability. They want to be reassured that deadlines will be met and that the consultants will be capable of delivering on time. The client will also want to be sure that there will be access to key people should a problem arise and that any such problems will be quickly resolved.

To establish reliability, the client will consult third party endorsements. Therefore, the more recommendations you have from past clients, the better. These will be especially useful if they come from clients in the same sector and relate to projects of similar complexity and value.

To supplement client endorsements, reliability can also be established by case studies and project profiles. These would demonstrate that you have the experience to deliver a service in a reliable way. Clients are, naturally, anxious to avoid being let down. That is why it is often difficult to win an appointment if there is already an incumbent consultant delivering a good service.

To convey your reliability you will need to demonstrate how you:

- monitor progress against a programme of deliverables
- can adapt quickly and accommodate change
- have a clear communications structure within your own team and how you communicate and monitor or control other consultants' input.

Some bid documents may specifically ask about these aspects but, if they do not and it is appropriate to do so, highlight these points.

Reasons why bids fail and the need to obtain feedback

Given the need to establish credibility, capability, compatibility and reliability, it is important to obtain feedback from clients on your bids, which will have the following benefits:

- providing the opportunity to improve your bid-writing skills since the more bids you submit and the more feedback you obtain, the more quickly you will enhance your technique and therefore your ability to submit winning bids
- gaining a better insight into how bids are evaluated
- possibly obtaining information about your competitors
- showing the client that you are serious about submitting a winning bid. Asking for feedback will also show the client that you are professional in your approach and are sincerely interested in submitting future bids
- advising those who contributed to the bid why the bid failed; this information should be conveyed in a constructive way rather than within a culture of blame.

There is also some benefit in obtaining feedback when you win a bid. There is always room for improvement and the request again shows the client that you are serious about continuous improvement.

In the case of a bid through an *OJEU* notice, there is an obligation on the client to give feedback. Therefore request a debrief feedback meeting with the client. Figure 3.3 gives

Dear Mr Contact

Re: Contract title

Thank you for your letter dated .... advising that we were not successful with our tender for the above contract.

We are always striving to improve our tender submissions and in so doing enhance our proposals so they reflect the client's needs in respect of service delivery and our ability to be competitive.

You will therefore appreciate that it is important for us to examine in detail the reasons for not being successful on this occasion. This will ensure that we continue to offer a service of excellence to our clients.

By addressing these points we will hopefully prove more successful in future opportunities, to the benefit of both of our organisations.

We would therefore welcome an opportunity to discuss our recent submission with you in detail at a time suitable to yourself. I will contact you in the next few days to make a mutually acceptable appointment.

Yours sincerely

FIGURE 3.3: Sample letter to the client requesting a feedback meeting

an example of a sample letter to the client requesting a feedback meeting. Private sector clients do not have an obligation to give feedback but, hopefully, if you explain your reasons and the potential benefits to the client, they will accommodate your request.

Many consultants who request a debrief meeting fail to prepare themselves with appropriate questions to ask and so may not uncover the real reasons for failure. The client, or their advisers, may simply offer feedback on the scoring of the bid, but you need to find out more than that.

During the debrief don't just look for the acceptable reasons for being unsuccessful, such as losing on price. Try to acquire feedback on things that really matter. Unfortunately, the client may not be willing to answer some of the more penetrating questions, at least not directly. Therefore try to explain to the client why you want to know. Let them understand that the feedback is valuable in establishing the appropriate level of service to offer, and possibly being able to provide a better price.

Here are some of the questions you should be asking, based on the key reasons why bids fail:

In respect of credibility	• How compelling was the proposed level of service being offered? • Were the client endorsements relevant and appropriate? • Were the examples of client benefits relevant, appropriate and of interest?
In respect of capability	• Were the examples of experience and track record relevant and appropriate? • Was the experience sufficient or was it lacking in any way? • Were the competitors more experienced? • Did the project profiles/case studies bring out the relevant capability to undertake the project under consideration? • Were there any deficiencies in the level of resources, technical ability and sector knowledge? How did these compare with the competitors' abilities? • Was there sufficient evidence in the bid document of using the team's experience to meet specific client needs? • Were any members of the proposed team perceived to be weak in any way?

In respect of compatibility	• Were there any issues with the approach to providing the service delivery? • Were any of the competitors better placed because they were already known to the client? • Was the bid document written in the appropriate manner using the client's/sector's language? Were there any elements of the bid document that were ambiguous or unclear? • Did the bid convey engagement with the client and other team members to achieve continuous improvement through initiatives such as 'lessons learned' and regular workshops?
In respect of reliability	• Did the team's structure and lines of communication demonstrate sufficiently that the team would be responsive to addressing and resolving problems or changes? • Did the client endorsements that were provided sufficiently address reliable delivery of the project in accordance with the brief and budget?
Other issues	• In respect of price, how did the bid compare with those of the competitors? Was sufficient information provided on what was included in or excluded from the price? • Were there any omissions from the bid? • Were any of the questions misinterpreted? • Did any of the competitors offer something which the client thought was better? • Was any irrelevant information provided in the bid? • Was there a lack of clarity or lack of key messages or benefits? • Was there a perception that some of the answers were of a generic nature rather than tailored to the client's specific requirements? • Was the style of the writing appropriate and easy to understand? • Is there anything else that could have been done better?

Careful consideration of any feedback obtained will help to determine if you have a good chance of winning similar projects in the future. If, on reflection, your chances of success are slim or non-existent, due perhaps to a lack of relevant experience, then it would be best to find an alternative opportunity to win work. To help in your decision-making process, it will be useful to employ some form of 'bid or no bid' process, as outlined below.

'Bid or no bid' decision

You need to focus all your efforts on the winnable bids. Don't waste your time on the long shots if better opportunities exist. Consider the probability of success and use some form of probability evaluation when following up leads and enquiries.

A good business development programme will have a 'pipeline' or a record of leads and enquiries. A lead (sometimes referred to as a prospect) is project specific. It is where an actual project is identified. It is not a client. Clients can generate many leads. A lead is the first stage in the pipeline. The client might not be aware of you at this stage or, if they are, they have not actually asked you to do anything. An enquiry is, again, project specific and occurs when the client has asked you to produce a proposal, price, initial ideas, etc.

As a guide, use probability success rates, where 100 per cent is achieved when a contract is signed. Leading up to this, at the lead stage consider the following levels of probability of success:

- an *OJEU* notice starts off at only 2 per cent unless you are known to the client and already know about the project
- in respect of other potential clients that don't know you (but where the prospect is not an *OJEU* notice), then this should not be more than, say, 10 per cent
- if you are known to the client, then the maximum probability should still be 20 per cent.

Probability of an enquiry being converted into a job:

- In the case of a tender, use statistics. If four competitors are tendering, estimate a 25 per cent probability of conversion unless you believe you have a better or worse chance than the others tendering.
- If nobody else has been asked to submit a proposal then it's purely the probability of the job going ahead. Start low and raise the probability every time you review the project and it seems to be progressing well. Or lower the probability if the project is not progressing or is likely to be cancelled.

How good is your relationship?

You must also take into account relationship values when considering the probability of success in converting leads to enquiries and enquiries to signed contracts. You might look at simple criteria in evaluating your relationship with the potential client, such as:

- hot (good relationship)
- warm (developing relationship)
- cold (little or no relationship).

Alternatively, expand the relationship classification to suit your requirements.

To assist your 'bid or no bid' decision it may be wise to have a checklist. Some of the points to consider are listed below:

Client details	• Who is the ultimate client?
	• Are we working as subcontractors?
	• Who will pay our fee?
	• Has the client any consultant advisers? If so, who are they?
	• Is the client knowledgeable about construction?
	• Is the client known to us?
	• Have we worked with this client before?
	• Does the client contact have authority to appoint us?
	• Does the client have previous construction experience or experience of working with consultants?
The competition	• Are we in competition?
	• How many competitors are there?
	• Are we competing against similar organisations?
Funding and fee	• Is funding for the project and fees in place?
	• What is the estimated contract value?
	• Is any speculative work required to win the project?
	• What will be the cost of speculative work, including expenses?
What is our probability of success?	Probability increases if:
	• the project is for an existing client
	• the project is in an existing sector of expertise
	• we are liaising directly with the client.
	Probability decreases if:
	• we are responding to an advert
	• the client hasn't worked with us before
	• we are subcontracted to someone else.

Increase your chances of success

Having decided to bid, you can increase your chances of creating a winning proposal by adopting the following measures.

Address the 3Cs + R test

Make sure that, wherever possible, you have given the client the reassurance of knowing that you are credible, capable, compatible and reliable.

Aim to achieve the highest score based on the evaluation criteria

Study the evaluation criteria and make sure that your submission will gain the highest score possible. Don't skimp on the high-scoring elements. Everything you write must be geared towards addressing the evaluation criteria. If you don't get the highest score, you don't win.

Address all the questions that the client may have

Read and reread your submission and see if you need to add any further detail or information to fully address all the questions that the client may have.

Use all the keywords from the client documentation?

You must use the client's terminology rather than your own. Make sure that every keyword is used and addressed. The evaluator of the proposal will be looking out for these words so make sure you have answered the question thoroughly. Often the evaluator will skim through the response looking out for the keywords. Make sure they are there and easy to find.

Ensure that each section passes the 'so what?' test?

Don't just make statements but take the time to say how they will benefit the client. Ask yourself 'so what?' about every statement you make. You need to elaborate and tell the client why the statements are important and how you will bring added value and additional benefits to the project.

Give the client reasons to select you

The client may have several proposals to select from. Have you given them compelling reasons to pick you? This means you really do need to understand what it is that the client wants, which may or may not be directly stated in the client documentation. Having identified the client's needs, then fully address them and explain how you will be fulfilling them.

► **SUMMARY CHECKLIST**

- Your proposal should satisfy the 3Cs + R test
- Use positive words and phrases
- Use facts and figures to substantiate your claims
- Research the client to make sure you are compatible and are able to demonstrate your compatibility
- Be ruthless in your 'bid or no bid' evaluation. Only pursue those opportunities with a good chance of success
- Think twice about submitting a bid when you are not known to the client. Take time to build up a relationship before the bid opportunity arises
- Write your proposals to specifically address the evaluation criteria. Aim to score high marks on each section

CHAPTER 4
Improving your chances of success through better understanding of your competitors

Is there a favourite already?

When considering whether or not to bid for a tender, it is important to establish whether the potential client is communicating with some of your competitors. Alternatively, there may already be an incumbent consultant, in which case you need to ask yourself what are the realistic chances of succeeding.

Before committing valuable time and resources to a bid, you should look for signs to suggest that a tender has been put together to favour one of your competitors. Here are some indicators to look out for which could suggest that the client already has a favourite:

- There appears to be an emphasis on certain aspects within the evaluation criteria in which only an incumbent, or a favourite competitor, will be able to achieve top marks. An overemphasis on very specific experience might also indicate this bias.
- The evaluation criteria may have an unusual bias. If cost is normally evaluated at 60 per cent on this type of project and on this occasion it is only being evaluated at 10 per cent you ought to wonder why.
- A short deadline might favour a competitor who is already expecting the tender documentation and has some inside knowledge of the project. The competitor might have put the tender package together on behalf of the client or might have been involved in the briefing stage, helping the client to define their needs.
- A requirement for a fixed price when insufficient information is supplied.
- Documentation within the tender incorporates work from a competitor.

Sometimes projects are developed through a multi-stage process. The client might have appointed a team to prepare the briefing document to incorporate within the tender package. This team may then be free to bid for the work in the subsequent tender process. They would have a distinct advantage in that they have already built up a relationship with the client and are familiar with both the project and the needs of the client. In these situations it may be difficult to win the tender.

How to win if there is a favourite

If you think that there is a favourite or an incumbent then you need to make your bid stand out. There is no point in merely being the same or slightly better than the favourite if you want to win. If you have evaluated your chances of success and you still believe there is a chance to win, then you may decide to be bold and try:

- being categorically different
- telling them a story that they want to be part of. Forget all your traditional approaches – be in their face!
- checking whether there is an incumbent and, if so, how they have been providing the service. Present a solution which, in comparison to the incumbent's, looks fresh and innovative, using current thinking and technology.

If there is an incumbent, focus on the service gap

Having undertaken your research and spoken with the client, you might have detected that the incumbent provider is not performing particularly well.

This could be for a number of reasons, such as:

- the incumbent has been paying more attention to winning new clients than to keeping current clients happy
- there have been delays, mistakes or poor quality work on current projects
- projects have been coming in over budget
- personality clashes may have arisen.

Alternatively, the incumbent might be delivering the promised service but, over time, the client has perceived that this service could be better. The client may have expected a continuous improvement in the service which hasn't materialised. Sometimes the incumbent might actually be delivering a good service but simply not keeping the client informed of the benefits provided.

This situation can continue until the client detects, or perceives, a service gap developing, as illustrated in Figure 4.1.

If you detect that the client perceives the level of service being provided by the incumbent to be inadequate, then you need to emphasise your strengths. Initially, concentrate on your strengths in areas which match the incumbent's weaknesses. So, if you are aware that projects have regularly come in over budget then show, giving examples, that your projects have kept within budget.

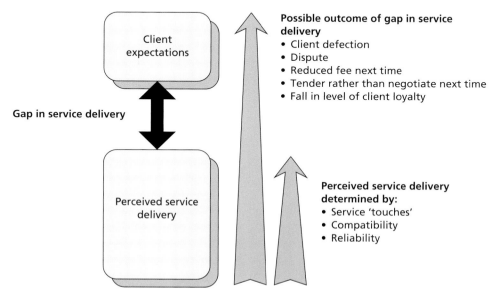

Client expectations determined by:
- Sales and marketing pitch
- Past experience
- Referral or reference

Client expectations

Possible outcome of gap in service delivery
- Client defection
- Dispute
- Reduced fee next time
- Tender rather than negotiate next time
- Fall in level of client loyalty

Gap in service delivery

Perceived service delivery

Perceived service delivery determined by:
- Service 'touches'
- Compatibility
- Reliability

FIGURE 4.1: Service gap

As part of the 'bid or no bid' considerations you need to evaluate whether the perceived service gap that has developed is sufficient to cause a client defection from the incumbent. It may be that the client is simply testing the market to see if a switch to a new provider is of any benefit.

What to do if you are the incumbent

You may already be working for a client and you are aware that there will be other projects but the client, for various reasons, has to put them out to competitive tender. Alternatively, you may be unsure whether the client will go to tender. The client might negotiate with you or ask you for a proposal, after which, they may go to tender if not totally convinced by your offering. So, what do you do?

The key thing is to be alert to signs that may indicate your current relationship is weakening. Have you noticed any subtle changes in your relationship with the client? Perhaps there have been problems along the way and you are not sure what view the client has taken on these. The worst thing you can do is be complacent. Don't just think you will win the next project because:

- the client knows and likes you
- you are the best, and your competitors don't have a chance
- the client will not want to experience the cost, hassle and potential risk of changing consultants
- it is already 'in the bag'.

Take time throughout your current project to meet the client and discuss your ongoing performance. Ask them for a 'wish list' of things they would like to do differently or add to the delivery performance. Possibly the best way of finding out what the client is really thinking is to schedule a neutral third party assessment (TPA).

The benefit of a TPA is that the client will find it easier to express opinions that they might not want to share with you directly. The TPA should be able to identify problems or issues that you were either not aware of or thought had been resolved. The exercise might provide further insights into your relationship with the client. It might, indeed, show that the client really does enjoy working with you. The very process of undertaking a TPA will show the client that you are actively engaged in ensuring their satisfaction. They will see that you are investing time, money and effort in your commitment to them. Also, what you may uncover and then address may improve your chances of winning the next bid. The feedback might help you to:

- improve your communications and performance
- counteract your competitors' advances, as they may have been knocking on your client's door
- generate ideas for innovation or mitigate trends that are pushing for change.

The best time to put a TPA in place is at least a year before your current contract ends. Better still, make a TPA part of your current contract schedule, beginning a few months after you have been awarded the contract and then recurring every six months or annually. What you must avoid is a sudden panic a few months before the contract ends and then starting to pitch for new work. The client will see through this. Better to show that you care from the outset. It takes so much effort to secure a good new client, so don't jeopardise the chance to win more work through not being seen to want to improve or enhance your service delivery.

If you still find yourself having to bid for work when you are the incumbent, then take time to implement the following strategies:

- Find out who else, apart from your current client contacts, might be driving the new procurement process. Then, once identified, set about finding out what their priorities and preferences are.

- If you have been given a pre-qualification document to complete then don't rely on your previous submission. What you are doing now may not be what the client wants in the future. Make your proposal look fresh, as if you are trying to win a new client. By all means remind them of all the good points of your current service provision. Also address any bad points so they are certain that your re-appointment will result in an enhanced service delivery.
- Answer the pre-qualification questionnaire properly and fully. Make your bid mirror what the documentation is asking for, not what you know 'they really want or need'. Too many incumbents tend to price for things that are not specified and consequently price themselves out of a job. Equally, don't tell the client that they are wrong or that they don't really know what they want. Obviously, if you know of certain specific requirements which they have not included in their documents you can mention in your documentation that you are aware of these, as long as this will not cause them embarrassment. For example, you might be aware that the client's employees are anxious about the new project, in which case you can emphasise how much effort you put into liaising with stakeholders to get them on board.
- Bid to win. Don't be complacent. You might even bring in outside help to prepare your bid in order to bring a fresh perspective to your established approach.

Compare yourself to the competition

When putting together a strategy for bidding for more work you may gain some insight into what to pursue and your chances of success by considering the tactics of your competitors.

- In what sectors do they compete? Do they specialise in one or two sectors?
- What size of contracts do they undertake?
- Are they more successful than you and, if so, why?
- What client portfolio do they have? Can you learn anything from how they operate to win bids?
- Have you lost to them before? If so, have you obtained client feedback?

By doing this research you will be able to undertake a competitor analysis similar to the one illustrated in Figure 4.2.

By undertaking a competitor analysis you will be better placed to consider your likely chances of success and this will influence your 'bid or no bid' decision. This would be especially true if you are bidding for work in a small geographical area and particularly on smaller work which would not attract the interest of competitors outside the area. On larger projects, or in an another area, you may not be aware of who the actual competitors will be.

Competitor	Coverage			Sector activity						Comments
	Local	Regional	National	Commercial	Industry	Health	Residential	Leisure/sport	Education	
LPA Design	X	X		X				X	X	• Well-established with good local and regional clients
Industry Design Group		X			X					• Only work within the industrial sector • Only one partner, have succession problems and associates leaving • Haven't worked locally yet but have been pitching for local work
Vision Design Ltd	X	X	X	X	X	X	X	X	X	• Large national business with good blue-chip clients • Have taken on new education specialist as partner • Have won many design awards
B & D Studio	X			X						• Mainly interiors and space planning • Senior partner is very well-connected and is expanding into other areas

FIGURE 4.2: Competitor analysis

On some projects, especially public sector ones, there may be an open invitation for interested parties to attend a briefing session. By going along to these you may be able to identify some of the competitors who are showing an interest. You will also be able to see what the likely overall interest is going to be and evaluate your chances of success accordingly.

As part of your analysis, undertake a SWOT analysis. This is where you take a hard look at your firm and identify what you believe are your strengths, weaknesses, opportunities and threats. Do this on a project-by-project basis. An example is shown in Figure 4.3. If you have detected a specific weakness early enough, see if you are able to address it. However, if your competition is far more experienced in the type of building being tendered for and this aspect is heavily weighted in the scoring, then consider whether it is really worth pursuing the tender.

Strengths	Weaknesses
• Our experience in commercial and industrial projects • Dedicated employees • Big enough to undertake both large and small projects • Good client portfolio • Gain many new clients through recommendations • Have a good interior design team	• Experience limited to two main sectors • As we grow bigger we might find it difficult to fit in the smaller projects for our established clients • Little experience with design and build projects • We have outgrown our office • Only one office location so can't offer good UK coverage • Poor succession planning
Opportunities	**Threats**
• Open up another office to serve large project recently secured and try to win further work in that area • Forge links with contractors in key sectors to undertake design and build work • Need to relocate our office to new premises to reflect our image • Develop our interior design capabilities to win major commercial refurbishment contracts	• Larger firms now looking to target our clients • Larger firms are investing heavily in new technology • Competitors forming links with larger contractors to secure design and build projects • Our best employees are always being approached by our competitors

FIGURE 4.3: An example of a SWOT analysis

Differentiate yourself from your competitors to increase your chances of success

Your competitors may be communicating with your target clients on a regular basis so there is a need to differentiate yourself. You must stand out from your competitors in some way. This might prove difficult but submitting a thoroughly bespoke document that addresses the client's specific needs will be a good first step and will greatly improve your chances.

In undertaking the competitor and SWOT analysis, try to identify anything you do that can help to set you apart. This could be your approach to a project, your experience or skill sets. Also, if you are able to identify specific benefits to the client from the service you are offering this would be an additional advantage.

It is very difficult to differentiate on price. If your message is that you are cheaper than your competitors then you may undermine your aim to be different. Of course, you may be cheaper or, shall we say, better value compared to competitors because:

- you are a multi-professional firm and so are able to provide all the required consultancy input and reduce overheads for the client's benefit
- you are expert in the client's sector and so have no need to go through a learning phase
- you have invested heavily in technology, which enables you to complete tasks more quickly and efficiently, thus offering the client savings
- you are local, thus saving on travel time when visiting the client and the site.

The other key point is to find what attributes the client prefers in their consultant. You might have identified these in your pre-tender discussions with the client. If you can identify these special attributes then present a key one, or several similar attributes, and try to differentiate yourself within your bid.

Should you discover, for example, that the client is extremely risk averse, you could address that in your bid by bringing out how:

- you have a specialist risk-avoidance champion
- you produce and regularly review a risk register on a wide variety of topics
- you hold workshops with the clients and other members of the team during the design and construction stages to make sure that the project is, and remains, within budget
- you take stakeholder management seriously and ensure that all the key people are on board with the project
- you have a strong commitment to in-house quality assurance procedures
- you invest in training to keep up to date in all aspects of risk management.

The key to effective differentiation is not to be all things to all people. You will need to change your bid documents to suit your specific target client. The skill lies in making the client believe you are a perfect fit and that you share the same values.

When you submit your bid, highlight the three key areas that go to the heart of addressing the client's needs. You are then well on the way to differentiating yourself and tailoring your bid to the client's needs. During the briefing stage, why not ask your client to pick out the three most important issues. Talk around each issue and see how you can shape your service correspondingly.

If you then need to expand each of the three points, try to find three ways to describe the benefits to the client. The power of three is a forceful tool.

Differentiate through customer service

The ideal situation is to acquire a level of competitive advantage that is sustainable over time and allows the client to perceive benefits during that time.

If you are able to differentiate yourself and appear to offer greater benefits than your competitors, other than price, then you will be able to:

- command a premium price for your service
- achieve better client loyalty
- win more work.

So, how can you improve your level of customer service so that it becomes a differentiating factor? Well, some of the areas you could tackle are:

- changing your culture so that it is client driven
- investing in good people – professional service firms 'sell' people, so your people need to be better than your competitors'
- investing in training – find out where there are weaknesses and train your people to excel
- promoting a positive culture
- appointing a client service champion
- trying to integrate the client into your organisation and teams
- delivering your promises
- striving to be the best.

Maximising your strengths and subtly revealing the weaknesses in your competition

During your competitor analysis you may uncover a particular strength you have when compared to your competitors. Or, alternatively, you may be able to positively differentiate yourself from various competitors in different ways. You can use this to your advantage.

You should never criticise your competitors but you can highlight their weaknesses by making a point of showcasing your strengths.

For example, one competitor may have a particular strength in the market sector being tendered. However, they are not local, so you could make a point of emphasising in your proposal the benefits to the client of having local knowledge.

▶ SUMMARY CHECKLIST

- Look out for signs that there is already a favourite consultant

- If there is a favourite, consider whether it is worth competing

- If competing when there is a favourite, then strive to differentiate yourself. Be categorically different

- If there is an incumbent consultant, investigate to see if there is a service gap. In your proposal, emphasise your strengths, which might just be the incumbent's weaknesses

- If you are the incumbent you will need to make a real effort to make your proposal look fresh. Don't be complacent and consider that the same service delivery will be satisfactory

- Consider a third party assessment to establish what the client really thinks about your service delivery

- Undertake a competitor and SWOT analysis

- Spend time on differentiating yourself from the competition

CHAPTER 5
Preparation and planning the process

Timetable and process

As soon as you are aware of the need to submit a proposal, pre-qualification or tender you need to start preparing.

Draft out a rough timetable based on your internal process and alert those people on whom you will be relying to contribute.

Within the process, allow time to:

- hold a readiness review to identify the areas, as far as is known, that have not yet been addressed or about which you have insufficient information
- check through all the research available to make sure you are ready when the tender or request for a proposal is published.

Contributors and team selection

As part of the preparation, make sure you have identified the contributors to the submission document or proposal as well as the person who will be in charge of its development.

You may also have to identify the delivery team, in which case make sure that those identified:

- are available to deliver the project
- are available to attend a pre- or post-tender presentation
- have up-to-date and bespoke CVs that are tailored to the client and their project.

Once the documentation is received, quickly review what is required in order to submit a compliant response. Check that all background and supporting information is available. If it is not, instigate the production of missing information, such as case studies and additional endorsements.

Keep the prospective client involved

To increase your chances of success and address all the relevant points you will need to keep the potential client involved during the preparation stage. If you are not submitting a tender but are putting forward a proposal document then consider:

- obtaining the client's approval to remain in contact during the proposal drafting stage to clarify points
- visiting key members of the client's team to go through various elements of the proposal at draft stage in order to obtain their feedback and build any relevant information into the proposal. It may be wise during this process to allow them the credit for some of the ideas
- issuing a draft proposal and meeting the client for a discussion and exchange of initial thoughts about the proposal
- encouraging comment and contribution from the client throughout the whole preparation stage.

However, if you are submitting a tender then consider the following points:

- Keep in touch with the client during the process by asking relevant questions regarding the project. You will need to be careful not to divulge your proposals or any key winning advantage you may have at this stage. The client will often be obliged to issue to all your competitors tendering copies of your questions and the client's answers.
- Try to be the first to ask the questions. This will show that you are enthusiastic and taking the process seriously. If you delay asking the key questions then the competitors may ask the same questions before you can and take the credit for doing so.

Process for preparing the document

Project intelligence and readiness review

Leading up to the release of the bid document you should constantly collect project intelligence. This might be from your client contact or other sources, such as the client's website. Keep in touch with the client, if possible, regarding the tender release date. You will need to know this so that you are fully prepared to start your submission without delay.

Armed with this information you will have the available time set aside for preparing the submission. If, in the meantime, another opportunity comes in, be prepared to abandon one opportunity to significantly enhance your success with another. Too many firms chase every project that they become aware of and then suffer by submitting weak proposals. Take a hard commercial view on the available prospects and always be ready to review the 'bid or no bid' position.

Documentation received and initial read through

Your first read through will be to check that:

- the project is still the same in scope as anticipated

- there are no show-stoppers, such as unacceptable contract terms
- any additional input required that wasn't anticipated can be accommodated in the time available.

Having reassured yourself that you still want to proceed, then do a second read through and start preparing bullet-point or brain-map replies to each question. Also, identify at this stage who might assist in writing the submission. As you are doing this you should also be considering what it will take to win the project. You will hopefully have a scoring matrix provided by the client (if a formal tender) or some client needs identified (if a proposal document). Based on this information you will know how to prioritise your effort.

You will need to prepare a bid timetable and send it to all those contributing with their individual deadlines highlighted. These deadlines should allow you sufficient time to edit and polish the contributions and present them in a consistent house style.

Team meetings

The size of the project and number of contributors, if any, will determine the need for team meetings. On larger projects there may be a need for an initial meeting to get an overview of the project, identify winning themes and reach agreement on commercial aspects.

Larger projects will also call for mid-point reviews and possible sign-off by senior management on certain commercial aspects.

Process, revision and reviews

When you revise and review the proposal document you need to:

- check the basics
- establish whether it answers the question
- ensure that it is compliant.

Check that you have included the extras, such as:

- client endorsements
- case studies and project profiles
- additional relevant information to differentiate yourself or gain additional marks.

Verify that:

- the proposal tackles what your client research has told you is required
- you have addressed the question of 'what will it take to win?'.

Depending on your resources, put in place a process (see Figure 5.1 for an example) that will help you with creating, revising and reviewing your proposal document.

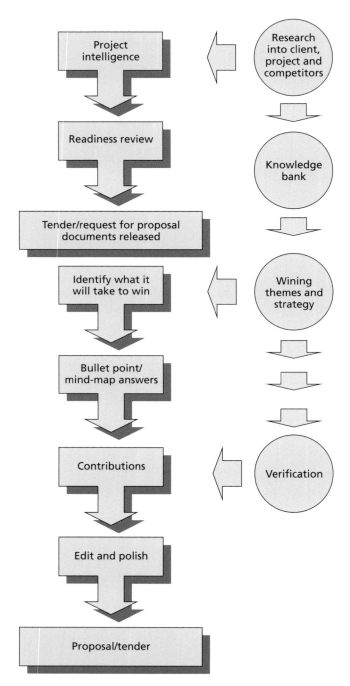

FIGURE 5.1: Create a process that works with your available resources

Themes and winning strategy

It is more likely that you will be able to develop themes within a proposal where you are setting the structure and content. Within a tender there will usually be a set structure to follow. However, there will be scope to develop themes within each section. These themes may be based on the information you have gathered in your pre-tender research.

How the 'bid or no bid' evaluation assists in the theme and winning strategy

If you have a robust 'bid or no bid' evaluation system, you will only be pitching for work that you have a good chance of winning. The selection process will assist you in deciding on the winning strategies to incorporate within your proposals.

If you consistently bid for opportunities from clients who are accepting proposals from all and sundry, then it will be difficult to position your business within the marketplace. If the project is particularly price sensitive then there may be no scope for you to provide a service that differentiates you from the next lowest price.

If your 'bid or no bid' strategy picks out the projects that meet your corporate strategies, core capabilities and strengths and allows you to differentiate yourself from the competition, then you will be able to put winning strategies in place.

To compile a winning proposal you need to create a story that the client wants to be part of. That story will position you favourably compared to your competitors. By only bidding for opportunities that reflect your corporate strategies, and where you have a competitive advantage, you can prepare your proposal knowing what story to tell.

Format and production

Consider the format and the production of the tender or proposal documentation. Make sure you comply with any restrictions, such as font size, word or page count and appendices.

Points to consider:

- apply your house style in respect of font; perhaps use your company colour for headings and bullet points
- create a hierarchy for headings and sub-headings and be consistent throughout
- use section dividers
- if the documentation runs to several binders, consider using a bespoke box to contain them
- use the client logo (if permitted) within the footer or header to make the documentation more bespoke

- use a binding that allows the open document to lie flat when being read
- use double-sided printing (showing consideration for your carbon footprint) and recycled materials
- make use of white space – do not overfill the page
- use graphics to make a point
- put additional information into an appendix and cross-reference it within the body of the submission.

If several questions ask for the same information then repeat it. Do not refer to another answer for support. With some larger projects the tenders are divided up and sections are sent off to different markers so you need to make sure that every answer can stand alone.

Creating a storyboard

It is worthwhile having a brainstorming session at the outset of the process of submission preparation. This might also be a good time to create a storyboard, which is simply an outline of the various parts of your proposal where you can list:

- the points that need to be addressed, which have been specifically requested
- any additional features and benefits that will help to differentiate your proposal from your competitors'
- extra applicable information, if time and resources permit.

Your storyboard will also need to incorporate a bid theme(s). This will be a theme or idea that you want the client to notice and which, hopefully, will set you apart from your competitors. Bid themes could include:

- innovation
- one-stop service delivery (if yours is a multi-professional firm)
- design capability (backed by design awards and media coverage)
- sector knowledge (this might be your niche sector).

Format if submitting a proposal

Unlike a tender, the proposal document may not be constrained by a defined format or specific need to answer particular questions. In that instance, the client may not be requesting a particular structure or format for your proposal. The proposal may have come about through discussions with the client and you are now taking the opportunity to address all the issues in one document. Therefore, if the client has not been specific about the structure or content of your proposal you might consider the following proposal format:

An executive summary	This should be a series of clear and unambiguous paragraphs, which will allow the client to get a feel for the key issues of the proposal.
Introduction	This section will set out the brief history leading up to the submission of the proposal, the outline of the assignment and how it has developed.
Putting the assignment in context	Use this section to address the issues that the client is facing. You will need to demonstrate your knowledge of the client's business and markets and the client's current business needs.
The solution to the client's needs and your ability to provide the service to meet those needs	Within this section you can outline any options you have considered. You will be able to discard some options (with reasons) and concentrate on describing the remaining options and providing recommendations. Hopefully, you will have had an opportunity to obtain feedback on the recommendations during your interaction with the client as part of the proposal development. You don't want to risk putting forward recommendations that may be rejected by the client. Use this section to demonstrate value for money, benefits and your strengths and unique ability to provide the solution. Also include, if possible, programmes and costings.
The delivery team	Put together a bespoke team to deliver the project. Do not include generic company structures. Show how the delivery team will be part of the client team and detail the lines of communication and what the various responsibilities will be. Include CVs that have been rewritten specifically for the project and that bring out specific skills and experience relevant to the assignment.
Appendix	Use the appendix to include the agreed brief, research, outcomes from workshops and visits, background information of your firm with appropriate examples of projects and endorsements from clients. Items in the appendix must be referred to in the main body of the proposal so that they are relevant and have a clear purpose.

Approach to fees at proposal stage

The client will want to have either an indicative fee or a fixed fee at this stage. You will only be able to provide a fixed fee if all the contract conditions concerning the provision of your services have been met. You may require independent advice from lawyers, advisers or your insurance providers. You may place a condition on your fee to state that it is purely indicative, based on documents received (and you may list the documents you have relied on) and on the final agreement on contract conditions. You would be wise to take legal advice, and advice from your insurers, on how to approach fee bidding and contracts for the provision of professional services. You will therefore need to think carefully about how to handle this issue, considering the following:

- It may be wise to link the indicative or fixed fee to a proposal or option within the proposal, making the proposal very specific in respect of the scope and duration of the project.
- If possible, leave the fee out of the proposal document if the proposal is being evaluated by a client team. You don't want your fees to be broadcast throughout the client's organisation and you will have no control over the document's circulation. If the fee is required at the proposal stage, then consider placing it within a separate document that can be handed to the appropriate client team member whose responsibility it is to negotiate the fee with you.
- Ask your client if you can submit a fee once there has been some official feedback on the proposal. It is best to submit a fee proposal once the preferred option has been identified and any changes accommodated or considered. See the proposal document as being stage one, with stage two being a submission on fees.
- If the assignment is straightforward, and once you have had some feedback on the initial proposal, you can expect to discuss fees in detail.

Consider incorporating a section confirming compliance, additional services and variations

Take every opportunity to differentiate yourself from your competitors. A good technique is to incorporate a section at the beginning of your submission which confirms that you have:

- complied with the client's requirements; particularly relevant if you have various options for services to be provided (for example, you may be able to offer additional skill sets)
- provided additional services
- considered alternative options
- offered additional elements which are either additional to or included within the fee.

A simple example is shown below.

Confirmation of compliant submission and additional points for consideration

Confirmation of service	We confirm that we will be providing the following professional services:
	• project management
	• architects.
Additional services available	If required, we are able to provide the following additional services:
	• interior design
	• landscape design.
	These services are available from within our organisation.
Additional service at no extra fee	We have included within our proposal interim value engineering workshops. We will manage the process and coordinate all aspects of the project with other team members, including the client and contractor when appointed.
Compliant proposal	Our proposal and fee submission reflect the services required as outlined in the client documents and further instructions arising from various meetings. Minutes of these meetings are contained in the appendix.
Options considered	In addition to our compliant proposal, we have considered:
	Option 1: reducing the phasing from five phases to three, which we believe will result in considerable cost savings and a reduction of the on-site activity from 18 months to 12 months.
	Option 2: the incorporation of off-site construction. To achieve this we have modified the original requirements slightly and this will result in a three-month reduction of the programme.
	These options are outlined in an additional section within our proposal.

If you are able to consider this approach at the outset, you can allocate the time and resources within your preparation process to considering options that might make you stand out from your competitors.

► **SUMMARY CHECKLIST**

- Prepare a timetable to reflect the input required and the available resources
- Identify the team and contributors and programme their contribution within the process
- Keep in touch with the client during the proposal/bid stage
- Hold a readiness review meeting and have interim team meetings if appropriate
- Consider themes and a winning strategy in conjunction with your 'bid or no bid' review process
- Consider preparing a storyboard and format for your submission
- If submitting a proposal, consider your approach to the inclusion of fees within the main document
- Consider incorporating a compliance section and highlight options considered

CHAPTER 6
Creating the document

The seven-step checklist on content – the 'must have' elements

This chapter details the key 'must have' elements to consider when creating a proposal or tender. When drafting and redrafting always keep these seven points in mind.

Step 1: Write the content to address the evaluation criteria

Look at the evaluation criteria and make sure you understand each element of them. Don't just rattle off the first thing that comes to mind. If you do, you then might not be answering the question fully, or perhaps not at all. Analyse the question word by word. Make sure you cover every aspect. There may also be other key information that could be relevant but which is, at first, not so obvious from the phrasing of the question.

You need to go for a maximum score on every question and every subsection of a question. There are no prizes for coming second. A good starting point on your first read through is to make a bullet point list or brainstorm chart of your answer (see Figure 6.1). The advantage of doing a quick brainstorming exercise is that you can come back to it later and add a few more points or strike out elements if they turn out not to be relevant.

Step 2: Do you pass the 'so what?' test (all about features and benefits)

Whenever you make a statement, take the 'so what?' test. What is the reason for making the statement and what are the client benefits? You may even need to ask the question several times. You must bring out features and benefits at every possible opportunity.

So, if you were describing your firm to a client in the education sector you might be tempted to say something along the lines of:

'We are one of the largest multi-professional consultancies within the UK.'

But, by asking yourself the 'so what?' question you may be able to enhance this by expanding it to:

'The fact that we are one of the largest multi-professional consultancies within the UK will have the following benefits for Broughton College:

- *we have a dedicated education team*
- *we have offices throughout the UK*
- *we work with specialist education advisors.'*

Then, by asking the 'so what?' question again, this becomes:

'Being one of the largest multi-professional consultancies within the UK, we can provide the following benefits for Broughton College:

- *We have a dedicated education team. They are fully up to date with current thinking in respect of how a college sports hall should be designed. This will ensure that Broughton College will have the most appropriate facility possible to meet its needs and budget.*
- *We have offices throughout the UK, with our nearest office located only a few miles away from Broughton College. This will enable us to react quickly to any on-site activity that needs our attention. This will give Broughton College confidence that should any problems arise, will be addressed and resolved quickly.*
- *We work with specialist education advisers. This gives us an insight into what the specific needs of Broughton College will be. In addition, it will enable Broughton College to benefit from best practice that has been developed at other sporting venues.'*

The above example is for a larger multi-professional firm, but the same approach could be used by smaller firms, as shown on the following page using a different format for maximum impact.

Continuing with the features and benefits theme, you can also highlight the benefits being offered to the client within your answers. Indeed, you could make a feature of them, as shown in the example below. This is particularly useful in catching the eye of the person evaluating your submission when they do a quick scan before the detailed marking.

Examples of features and benefits provided by a smaller professional services firm

Features	Benefits
We are a small firm	Your project will be very important to us and we will have a dedicated director/partner running the assignment. This will make sure that your needs are addressed as they arise.

We specialise in your sector and building type	As a consultancy firm, we excel in what we do. To achieve this we specialise in your sector and the building types within your sector. Whatever project you assign to us, we will have a team available that has experience of the particular building type. This minimises the learning process and gives the client the benefit of current best practice within the sector. This will also reduce costs and time and enhance the quality of the project to the appropriate standard.
We are a regional practice with one office that is local to you	This will enable us to manage the project locally. With the benefit of local knowledge, we will have experience of local contractors and suppliers. This will save money and be more efficient. Also, we will be able to service your needs more economically. These savings will be passed on to the client.
We are part of a benchmarking group	This gives us the opportunity to compare the various parts of the service with similar organisations throughout the UK. We are then able to address our weaker areas and build on our strengths. This approach gives the client a better service and the comfort of knowing that we are always improving the ways in which we operate and deliver our service. This status makes us more efficient, with the consequent savings being passed on to our clients.

First of all, brainstorm your answer, perhaps using a brainstorm chart. The sample question in Figure 6.1 is addressed in the brainstorm chart in Figure 6.2.

Your approach to service delivery
Explain, within 750 words, how you would organise your service to help deliver this particular school project to the client?

FIGURE 6.1: Typical question regarding service delivery

The answer could follow the following format. Notice how the benefits are highlighted in text boxes.

Our service is delivered in three distinct phases

In broad terms, we would organise our service to help deliver this particular school project to the client through three distinct phases. These are:

- *briefing (stakeholder engagement and visioning)*
- *pre-construction (design stage) and*
- *project delivery (construction stage).*

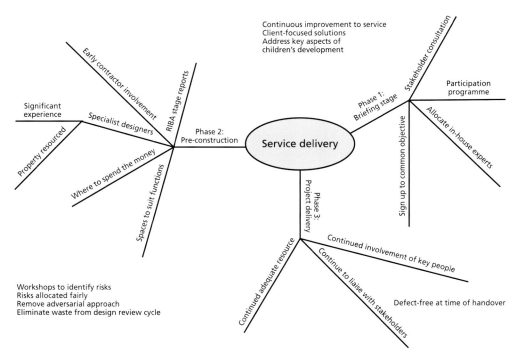

Continuous improvement to service
Client-focused solutions
Address key aspects of
children's development

Early contractor involvement

RIBA stage reports

Significant
experience

Specialist designers

Property resourced

Where to spend the money

Spaces to suit functions

Phase 2:
Pre-construction

Service delivery

Phase 1:
Briefing stage

Stakeholder consultation

Participation
programme

Allocate in-house experts

Sign up to common objective

Phase 3:
Project delivery

Continued adequate resource

Continue to liaise with stakeholders

Continued involvement of key people

Defect-free at time of handover

Workshops to identify risks
Risks allocated fairly
Remove adversarial approach
Eliminate waste from design review cycle

FIGURE 6.2: Brainstorm chart the answer

Each of the three phases requires the appropriate team members, with the distinct skills and experience needed for the successful completion of the phase. Also, each phase will be resourced to meet the project programme.

Phase 1: Briefing phase

We undertake extensive stakeholder and user consultation, which helps to clarify visions and identify briefs. We will organise formal and informal participation programmes to underpin our design process. We will also allocate our in-house experts, who will have the skill sets to resolve complex, possibly conflicting, stakeholder requirements and help to manage expectations.

Engaging with stakeholders enables the end users, in particular learners, teachers and community members, to make a significant contribution to the outcomes of a school design project. We will therefore aim to have everybody on board, pursuing a common objective.

> *Client benefits*
>
> *As part of our service delivery, during the briefing stage we will collaborate with the client, stakeholders and other design team members. The importance we place on collaboration allows us to continuously improve our service and deliver client-focused, coordinated solutions.*
>
> *With a well-developed brief, we will enter the next stage fully equipped to design a school that addresses the key aspects of the children's development, learning and well-being.*

Phase 2: Pre-construction

During this design stage we allocate our specialist designers, who are able to select materials for robustness, beauty and appropriateness. Our designers will make the structure and fabric of our buildings 'work hard'.

We believe that part of the skill of being an architect is in understanding 'where to spend the money'. The internal spaces will suit their functions, which will be adaptable to changing needs. The spaces will also have the desired interrelationships with adjoining spaces.

Our dedicated team will also have significant expertise in complex procurement and contractual administration processes, allowing us to provide substantial support to the client, both directly and as part of a project team. The project will be properly resourced with direct senior management input and a highly experienced, committed team. Our team is able to meet the most challenging design and programme demands.

We will work through RIBA Stage Reports, with client sign-offs clearly identified. Our service delivery will provide a hands-on, problem-solving approach via workshops held with other consultants, clients and stakeholders.

We would also encourage the early involvement of the appointed contractor so that the project can benefit from their input.

> *Client benefits*
>
> *Our methodology of service delivery during this stage would incorporate workshops. These workshops would allow the early identification of risks, which can then be evaluated and, where possible, designed out or mitigated.*
>
> *The management of the project-specific risks would be shared jointly by the client, design team and contractor. We would also seek to remove any adversarial approaches by the early engagement of the main contractor, giving the team common goals.*
>
> *This early involvement of the contractor would bring construction expertise into the preliminary design stages. This eliminates waste from the design review cycle, giving safer, more predictable construction. In addition, cost and value for money would feature as key items on the workshop agenda.*

Phase 3: Project delivery

Our service team will have discharged most of their responsibilities during the design stage. We will take through into the project construction stage one of our key senior architects. He or she will have specific on-site skills and, in particular, project management abilities. Our senior architect will have the necessary resource back-up to meet any demands that may occur during this phase.

This phase will feature our contract management skills and will make sure that the school is delivered to the correct quality of workmanship. We will continue our communications with the stakeholders and keep them fully informed of progress and, wherever possible, arrange site visits for them.

Liaising with the rest of the team, we will carry out regular inspections, which will deliver a zero-defects facility at the time of handover.

> *Client benefits*
>
> *The client will receive a school that is not only defect-free at the time of handover but will be on time and within budget. Having a defect-free building at handover will mean no disruption to the school activities after handover.*

We also include the CVs of our bespoke team for this project, which will be led by Clive Jones, director, and supported by Hugh Smith, one of our senior associates.

Step 3: Address all the issues the client may have

When preparing your answer, consider the reason behind the question. Is there a purpose for asking the question? Has the client been caught out before? Try to get behind the questions and see them from the client's point of view. Use the well-known Kipling poem to remind you to address the what, why, when, how, where and who.

I keep six honest serving men

(They taught me all I knew)

*Their names are **What** and **Why** and*

***When** and **How** and **Where** and **Who**.*

A useful technique when preparing your answer is to examine the question by:

- highlighting the elements of the question that ask for evidence of ability, your method of delivering the service and any other points to consider
- also, examine the client documentation to see what other information you have been given which helps to address the question being asked
- draft out key points that you consider need to be included within the answer.

As an example, this technique is used to address the question posed in Figure 6.3.

The elements of this question can be divided into:

- the ability to deliver (highlighted in bold text)
- what we can deliver (highlighted by underscoring)
- additional points (highlighted by use of italics).

Your current capacity to deliver the appropriate level of service

---

Provide evidence of your **capability and resource capacity** to manage, coordinate and deliver the appropriate level of service for this complex building *concurrently with your other workload.*

FIGURE 6.3: An example of a question regarding level of service

Therefore, the rough initial outline approach to the answer could be:

Key points to address	Points to mention
Ability to deliver	• Our track record of delivery • Include client references involving similar project type, complexity and size • Provide a resource schedule for the project and details of named individuals on the project, confirming their availability
What we can deliver	• Provide CVs of the team members and identify those that will manage, coordinate and deliver the project at the various design phases and during construction • If space permits, put in our methodology for managing, coordinating and delivering a service. Include how we manage and coordinate other consultants in the team and how we liaise with the client and stakeholders • Mention how we accommodate and handle changes in the design • Emphasise the team members' individual skills and experience specific to this project • Highlight our ability to deliver complex buildings and emphasise this within individual CVs • Provide a schedule of complex building work undertaken that is similar in nature to the current project
Additional points: other workload	• Schedule our other workload and the anticipated resources required • Show that the selected team for this project is available at the appropriate time • Schedule workload handled year on year, linking to resource availability to prove that we have managed in the past to deliver this volume of projects

In reality, the above format would be lengthier and would also include details of the individuals who would be tasked with contributing the various sections of the answer and the applicable deadlines.

Step 4: Use the client's language

Focus on the client's language. The documentation will have certain key words and these may be mentioned more than once. When reading through, highlight these key words and make sure you use them in your answer.

The person evaluating your answer may initially skim through your document before beginning a detailed evaluation. If they see familiar words they will be reassured and may be more inclined to give you high marks. You may even wish to put some of your answer in bold text or include the key words in sub-headings.

Consider the reader and how they may wish the information to be formatted

The process of presenting a successful proposal involves winning over each and every member of the evaluation team, especially the key decision makers. Remember that the key to a successful proposal is not to only focus on what you are able to do but to highlight what the client needs and how you will be able to satisfy those needs.

If your proposal or tender is being considered by just one person, then your task is easier as you will have (hopefully) some idea of their particular preferences regarding the formatting of the document. Sometimes the format is predetermined by requiring you to fill in boxes with strict word counts. On other occasions, especially in the case of a proposal document, you may have more freedom regarding the presentation of the submission.

The important point to appreciate is that each individual that may be reading your proposal or tender will have a different set of needs. Needs can be influenced by the individual's role within the business, the internal politics and relationships with other members of the client's organisation.

Different people like to receive information in different formats. Knowing your client's preferences will help to convey your message in a way that will be readily understood.

Consider the reader's personality and role and use these to your advantage

Those evaluating your proposal will have different characteristics and personalities. If you can reflect this fact in your documentation you will begin to build up a rapport. This will be to your advantage. If you have a chance to meet the client who will be evaluating your proposal, look out for the characteristics listed below. If several people are making the evaluation, then perhaps consider all of them. You might write different sections with certain evaluators in mind. It could be, for example, that the finance director will be looking at the costs and fees section, while the managing director will focus more on the final result and how that could enhance the company brand or status. A typical client may have the following types of people on board (these are very general statements and listed simply to raise awareness of possible characteristics):

Personality type	Points to consider in your documentation or when dealing with them during the proposal process
Director/leader/manager (e.g. managing director, project manager)	Generally they: • are bad listeners • want it done yesterday • talk in short sentences • are very competitive • like risk and change. So when dealing with them: • be concise • have all the answers • be different • make them feel important • inspire them • appeal to their status.
Socialiser (e.g. marketing or business development director)	Generally they: • like the big picture • are good at speaking • hate detail. So when dealing with them: • be sociable • don't bore them with detail • use visuals but not too many facts and figures.
Relater (e.g. human resources director/ manager)	Generally they: • are a team person • like to meet team objectives • like to say 'yes'. So when dealing with them: • make them feel part of the team • outline team or project objects • give them opportunities to agree and say 'yes'.

Thinker (e.g. finance director, research director, IT director)	Generally they: • like data • are overly analytical • are tidy • like systems and procedures • are conformist. So when dealing with them: • give them the detail • use graphs, statistics and charts • deliver the information in a well-structured, procedural way.

Some people will not fit easily into the above categories or might appear to be a mixture of several types. The key point is to become aware of how your client likes to receive information. If you make it easy for them to understand your proposal and they enjoy reading it, then you have a better chance of success.

Step 5: See your answer from the client's point of view

As often as possible, use the client's name, the name of the project or its location. Make it totally bespoke. Don't give the evaluator any reason to think that you have just copied and pasted from another answer. If you do use your name or company name, use it to describe how you will bring the client benefits. For example:

> *'ABC Design Studio has designed many educational buildings'*

becomes

> *'With our experience within the education sector we believe that ABC Design Studio **fully understands the requirements of Broughton College**. We have analysed the outline accommodation requirements for the new sports hall and are confident we will design the project on time, within budget and to the desired quality. We have designed ten sports halls of a similar size and completely understand the demanding needs of your project. Our experience will help us to focus on and design your sports hall to your specific needs and reflect the demanding issues of the site and adjoining properties.'*

Content influenced by the type of client

The way that you package your message in your documentation may be determined by what you know about the client. It is a great advantage to know the level of the reader's technical understanding so that you can clearly outline your proposal at the appropriate level.

If your client is:	Consider:
Knowledgeable and impartial	Be prepared with all your supporting evidence. This type of client will want to be treated as knowledgeable and will want you to have considered and covered all the main points.
Less knowledgeable	They may be inclined to hear just the solutions rather than to dwell upon the potential problems.
Sympathetic	You might be able to give a more motivational delivery using more colourful language. This may be the case if you are the incumbent consultant and there is no competition. Be careful, however, that you do not become complacent. You will still need to cover all the points and come up with good solutions or recommendations.
Hostile	You need to build up your credibility early on and be able to rely on evidence to back up your statements (client endorsements and project profiles that show added value and benefits to clients). This may be the case where there is already an incumbent consultant in place or you are aware that the client has a favourite and it is not you.

Step 6: Create a reason to select your proposal

You might be competing against other similar organisations, so you will need to differentiate yourself and provide compelling reasons why you should be selected.

To be able to do this you really need to know what the client's requirements are, and not simply those listed in the documentation. Have you carried out research? Do you have any inside intelligence? It's not good enough merely to address the issues raised. You must demonstrate that you have sufficient knowledge to be able to solve all the client's issues, even those that are not declared.

You must enhance your offering – be more efficient, quicker, better value for money, etc.

Step 7: Be compliant

You must stick to any conditions imposed within the document. These may include:

- word or character count
- font and font size
- no appendices, or specific limitations regarding their use
- no exclusions.

Writing an executive summary

An executive summary is typically a short summary of a long document providing a quick overview.

The executive summary gives the reader the main contents of the document in a nutshell. It will be the first part of the document the reader will read. It might be the only part that senior people within the client organisation will read. Therefore great care needs to be taken in its preparation.

Write the summary after you write the main report. Some people hold the view that the executive summary can, and should, be written first. This, they argue, gives structure to the rest of the document. By all means, draft an outline executive summary initially, but the final version should be prepared only when the whole document is complete.

The executive summary should be no more than one-tenth of the length of the main proposal. To write the executive summary you should:

- list the main points that the summary will cover in the same order as they appear in the main proposal
- write a simple sentence for each of the main points
- add supporting or explanatory sentences as needed, avoiding unnecessary technical material and jargon
- use bullet points to improve the presentation, where appropriate
- incorporate important facts and figures and introduce your bid theme
- establish the need or problem and demonstrate your knowledge of the key issues
- incorporate solutions and explain their value (benefits)
- finish with main conclusions and recommendations.

The executive summary is a powerful element within proposals and will give the reader a quick impression of your suitability and ability to undertake the assignment.

Principles of clear writing

Being clear in your writing will help to convey your message and will enhance your chances of success.

Some key points to improve your text are given below:

- know the difference between features and benefits and bring out the benefits of all your features
- limit sentences to a maximum of 20 words and vary the sentence length
- paragraphs should be a maximum of six lines long

- use headings to signpost the main topics and sub-topics
- avoid using negative words
- incorporate bullet points to break up the text
- incorporate graphics and quotes to vary the text and to reinforce a given point
- turn questions into answers.

Avoid being sidetracked when writing

When writing an answer to a tender or pre-qualification question, make sure you don't drift away from the key message. It is so easy to write copious copy on a subject that is not really addressing the point required.

To help you to address the question and not to go off topic, consider the following technique of breaking the answer into stages.

Stage 1: Prepare a structure for the answer.

Stage 2: When reading the question, highlight the key points then produce a bullet point (or brainstorm chart) draft. Refer to this when you review your answer.

Stage 3: Flesh out your draft answer, bullet point by bullet point.

The outline answer to Figure 6.4 demonstrates the techniques.

Proposed measures for service delivery
Outline your proposed measures for service delivery in line with the principles set out in the *Accelerating Change* report chaired by Sir John Egan.

FIGURE 6.4: An example of a question regarding service delivery

Structuring the answer

Introductory point

Accelerating Change is the most important report to have come out of *Rethinking Construction* and the Strategic Forum for Construction since the publication of the Egan Report in 1998.

- Say why.
- Say that you will be outlining the principles and how your measures, in line with those principles, will be of benefit to the client.

Second point: what are the principles?

Accelerating Change incorporates an improvement agenda and looks at several cross-cutting issues, as detailed below:

- Improvement agendas

  Accelerating Change focuses on the three improvement agendas of:

  A.   client leadership
  B.   integrated supply teams
  C.   people issues.

- Cross-cutting issues
  There are also several cross-cutting issues identified by the report and these include:

  - sustainability
  - design quality
  - IT and the internet
  - R&D and innovation.

Bullet point the whole answer

Go through each of the elements you have identified (e.g. client leadership).

- Bullet point all the individual measures under this point and do the same for all the other points.

Now go though each element of the answer and, using your bullet points (or brainstorm chart), prepare a first draft.

When you have drafted your answer then put it into the layout and style that has been set for your submission.

Layout and style

Use a structuring method

Picking out the key elements of the text to assist in conveying the message is critical in helping the reader to:

- scan the message
- be able to get a quick overview of the message
- identify how the message is being developed
- make a quick judgement on the quality and appropriateness of the message
- read individual sections and understand the context of the section within the whole.

Three-part method

If you receive various contributions for your document from team members you will need to edit them so that the whole submission is consistent in format and style. A good technique to use when editing contributions is the three-part method, which places the various elements into three categories. You could also highlight the text as you read through your team contributions. The three elements are:

- `headline facts`, such as project and client name, and **sub-headings** to break up the text (the sub-headings will cover different topics)
- *the features*: this element covers any technical descriptions and factual statements as well as descriptions of projects and key challenges
- the benefits: this element covers how the features delivered a benefit or how you propose to provide benefits. It also incorporates client endorsements.

The following original text serves as an example of the type of contribution you might receive from a team member.

`The new office building` *is located next to the existing company headquarters.* `The client, World Video Games Ltd,` *was occupying an old manor house which did not lend itself to being extended but we were able to build within the courtyard. The existing courtyard consisted of several temporary-looking buildings and was not of any recreational use as it was constantly in the shade. Access to the courtyard was difficult for traditional construction methods so it was decided to* `design a facility that could be built off site` *and lowered into place by crane.* This also enabled the construction programme to be reduced by two months compared to traditional construction methods.

The new office building was set apart from the existing office accommodation so as not to impact on existing views out. *The new building was linked by a fully enclosed covered way to the existing building.* This allowed the staff to move from one building to another without having to go outside. *The link corridor has a pitched roof, with the south-facing slope incorporating solar panels along its entire length.* `The power generated` *by these solar panels, the ground heat pump and turbine set in the grounds supplies* all the power needs of the new and existing buildings.

Unlike the existing building, the new office has been `designed to be open plan` *which allows for maximum flexibility to rearrange the workstation layouts to suit any future changing needs. Unfortunately, the existing building does not lend itself to an open-plan layout and the client wanted to maintain the cellular accommodation as this was now going to be used mainly as* `meeting and training rooms`.

This now becomes:

New open plan office accommodation for World Video Games Ltd

The new offices for World Video Games Ltd have just been completed and are situated in parkland next to the current headquarters building. The new offices are sufficiently far away from the existing offices not to obstruct existing views out.

The new facility has been designed as open plan to give maximum flexibility to the work station layouts. This also permits easy reconfiguration depending on, and to suit, the changing future needs of the client.

Existing building becomes a conference and training centre

The existing offices, which were originally an old manor house with a courtyard, did not lend themselves to an open-plan layout. This, in fact, suited the client as he will be using the refurbished building for meetings and as a training centre.

Modern off-site construction reduces building programme

With difficult access to the courtyard, it was decided to build a facility off-site and to then lower it into place by crane. This resolved the issue of access and also reduced the construction programme by two months, compared to traditional methods. The courtyard, which was only occupied by temporary buildings, provided additional space for office accommodation. With the courtyard being almost permanently in shade, there was no loss of external recreational space.

Sustainable features supply all on-site power needs

A new enclosed corridor links the new facility with the old. This allows the staff to pass between the two without having to go outside. The link corridor has a pitched roof and the entire south-facing pitch incorporates solar panels. Additional sustainable features include a ground heat pump and wind turbine set in the grounds. Together, these features generate all the power needed by the new and existing facilities.

Patterns, signposts and bridges

To keep the client's attention when reading your document, you will need to break down the main content of your presentation into small chunks of information. As you format your document, try to arrange your points into a pattern which will help to persuade your client. If you are not given a set format, then consider the following options:

- setting out the problem, discussing options and putting forward a recommended solution – this is the most common approach

- a chronological series – this might be useful if the project's development history is significant
- setting out a theory and then explaining how it would work in practice – this is useful if considering a new approach or referring to other projects which demonstrate a point or an idea that you are trying to promote
- using topics – you could commence your proposal by saying that there are three main issues and then go through them one by one
- a theme – you could relate your presentation to, say, a journey from A to C via B. This is a possible format if looking at a large development which may have a number of phases.

When reading your document, your client may need help to understand your thought processes. In these situations you may wish to create signposts to tell them where you are in those thought processes. You might, for instance, say:

'There are three main areas. First ... second ... and finally.'

This helps the client to orientate themselves within the proposal and provides a structure that is easy to understand. Understanding goes a long way towards persuading.

When you pass from one topic to another, or from one major section of your proposal to another, you may find bridging techniques useful, such as:

'Having dealt with the key areas of the brief, we would like to move on and explain how we intend to deliver a project that is totally compliant.'

Or

'We have outlined the key issues for this project and now we would like to discuss the key solutions.'

These bridges form a smooth transition and also help the reader to understand that you have concluded one section and are about to embark on the next.

Using lists, tables and graphics

It is a good idea to incorporate lists, tables and graphics within the proposal document so as to:

- break up long sections of text
- make a point easier to understand
- emphasise a point being made.

However, you need to:

- make sure they are relevant

- ensure that they are clearly labelled and make them brief
- consider whether they are entirely necessary in the main body of the text or should be put into an appendix
- consider using a summarised graphic, list or table that can be placed in the main body of the text with the bigger, more detailed version in the appendix
- make sure that all the lists, tables and graphics are in the same style. Too often, if these are cut and pasted in from other submissions, they are in different fonts or styles. If you are not careful you will destroy the bespoke nature of the submission
- use an easily legible font style within the graphic or chart
- put the graphics adjacent to the relevant text
- keep graphics small and compact – they will look better.

▶ **SUMMARY CHECKLIST**

- When creating the document, use the seven-step checklist in respect of the 'must have' elements
- Where appropriate, include an executive summary
- Make sure your content is clear, easy to read and unambiguous
- To avoid being sidetracked and drifting off topic, use the three-stage method
- Take time over the layout and style of your content. Consider using the three-part method to home in on the headline facts, features and benefits

CHAPTER 7
Using appendices

When to use an appendix

Appendices are used for supporting material which, if incorporated within the body of the bid, would make it poorly structured or too long and detailed. Intelligent use of appendices can convert an average submission into a winning proposal.

The appendix should be used for helpful, supporting or essential material that would otherwise clutter, break up or be distracting in the main text.

Points to consider are that:

- the central topic should be addressed in the main body of the document
- any supporting arguments should not depend on information contained within the appendix
- the appendix should not be used for information that could not be conveniently accommodated in the main text
- summarise the content of the information contained in the appendix within the main text and cross-refer to the appendix.

Appendices may include some of the following:

- printed material asked for in the tender, such as company accounts
- CVs
- case studies and project profiles
- supporting evidence and contributory facts
- copies of company policy statements
- award certificates, registrations and memberships
- specialised data (raw data appear in the appendix, summarised data appear in the body of the text)
- technical figures, tables or descriptions
- questionnaires (questionnaire results appear in the body of the text).

The body of the text must be complete without the appendices and it must contain all the information, including tables, diagrams and results, necessary to answer the question.

Appendices are not usually included in the word count. Therefore, the appendices can sometimes be used to include information that would take the main text over the word or page limit.

Appendices must be referred to in the body of the text; for example, 'further details of the project are given as a project profile in Appendix D'.

The following is an example of using an appendix to maximum effect when the main question (see Figure 7.1), within the bid documents, limits your answer to a specific word count. You need to be sure that the bid permits additional supporting information to be included within an appendix.

Training
What is your approach to providing training to your employees?

FIGURE 7.1: Typical question that would benefit from supporting documentation in an appendix

The answer might be along the lines of:

All our employees, at their annual assessment, discuss and agree their training plan for the forthcoming year. This plan consists of areas that the employee is keen to explore and training which is felt to be appropriate by their line manager.

All of our technical staff undertake continuing professional development (CPD) as set out by the RIBA. Currently, the CPD curriculum focuses on ten topics. In addition to this, we:

- *hold monthly lunchtime meetings where external speakers talk about technical issues*
- *attend external seminars*
- *arrange visits to recently completed buildings within the region*
- *support individuals who wish to obtain further qualifications*
- *occasionally hold joint training sessions with some of the other consultants we work with.*

Our support staff are also encouraged to undertake training in the latest software packages so that we are totally up to date with the latest technology to assist in the provision of excellent client service.

See also:

Appendix 1: Approach to training

Section A1: Standard agenda for our annual employee assessment

Section A2: Details of the RIBA CPD programme and ten topics covered

Section A3: Schedule of lunchtime talks for the past year and arranged for the next six months

Section A4: Schedule of training undertaken by support staff.

From the above, it can be seen that the question is fully answered with back-up supporting detail given in four sections within an appendix. The supporting documentation is referred to in the answer. Many consultants answering this question might not think of providing the supporting documentation. This might be because they do not have the documentation to hand or believe that such information would be excessive. But including such information gives credibility to the answer and shows a professional approach to training provision. By asking such a question, the client is clearly looking to check that the consultant is up to date with regard to current technology and regulations and is investing in employee training. As long as the information is relevant and adds to your submission, then place all the supportive information within an appendix. No matter how minor the question, you must remember that you want to score as highly as possible. An additional percentage point could make the difference between winning and coming second.

Make an appendix appropriate

When deciding what to place within the appendix, consider the reader or evaluator. The whole purpose of putting together a tender or proposal is to win the project.

We have mentioned before that we need to make our documentation as bespoke as possible. Therefore, only include within the appendix information that:

- supports the main body of the submission
- has been specifically requested, such as company accounts and CVs
- is referred to within the main body of the text.

If you do not work within these guidelines and use the appendix section to incorporate all your standard marketing material, you run the risk of:

- devaluing the bespoke nature of the submission
- the reader or evaluator skipping through the appendices and making the judgement that they are not relevant and thereby perhaps missing some vital information.

Format

When formatting the appendix, consider the following points:

- the heading should be APPENDIX or Appendix, followed by a letter or number (e.g. APPENDIX A, Appendix 1). It would also be useful to name the appendix with a descriptive title, for example 'Appendix B: Company Accounts'

- each appendix must begin on a new page
- appendices must be listed in the table of contents (if used)
- the page number(s) of the appendix/appendices will follow on from the body of the text
- follow the style of the main body of the document (in terms of font, heading hierarchy, etc.).

Content

When putting content into the appendix remember to make it relevant and bespoke. Sometimes the reader might not grasp the relevance or benefits of the information, so it might be useful to have a box panel at the foot of each appendix and head it 'the benefits of [insert the topic of the appendix] to [insert the client or project name]'.

Example of an appendix

Appendix G: Wren Barry Architects' commitment to training

We recognise the importance of training and we provide our employees with a range of internal and external training modules to suit their, and the company's, needs.

Training days

Over the past year, we have provided 67 training days, which covered:

- Technical aspects   8 days
- Management   3 days
- IT skills   22 days
- Additional qualifications   23 days
- External courses   11 days

In addition, we have held nine lunchtime CPD sessions.

Mentoring

We also have a mentoring scheme in place, which covers:

- those employees who have requested mentoring during their annual review
- all new graduates joining the company
- all employees who have been promoted.

Client and other consultant involvement

We also involve some of the consultants we work with, as well as clients and contractors, in joint training initiatives. Recent examples include:

- collaborative working (with other consultants, contractors and clients)
- creating a zero-defects culture (with contractor)
- how to get the most out of 'lessons learned' workshops (with consultants and contractor).

Benefits for County Council Construction services framework

The clear benefits to the framework from Wren Barry Architects' commitment to training are:

- having a team that is up to date on current legislation and technical advances relating to building design, which will enable the project to be designed to meet current requirements first time in the most cost-beneficial way
- individual team members will perceive that they are valued, which improves their workplace quality perception. This, in turn, will be reflected in improved quality performance to the overall benefit of the framework.

This example shows a level of detail which would be too much to include within the body of the submission. The panel showing the benefits to the client will reinforce the relevance of the appendix content to both the project and the client.

▶ **SUMMARY CHECKLIST**

- Supporting documentation should be placed in an appendix
- Summarise the content of the information contained in the appendix within the main text and cross-refer to the appendix
- The body of the text must be complete without an appendix
- Make the appendix appropriate
- Include a 'benefits' box to highlight the benefits to the client

CHAPTER 8
Showing off past projects

The need to demonstrate skills, experience and capability

To win a bid you will need to differentiate yourself from your competitors. One of the key ways to achieve this is to be able to demonstrate your experience and ability to successfully complete the project. You will need to show that your experience is applicable in that you have successfully completed buildings of the same type and of similar values. This should be seen as the basic minimum requirement unless the project is so unique that there are no comparable projects.

There will also be a need to demonstrate how your firm provided some added value to past projects. You may have been innovative, with resultant savings in time and cost. Alternatively, you may decide to emphasise other aspects of your input which, from your research and pre-bid enquiries, you know will be of particular interest to the client.

The easiest way to demonstrate your skills, experience and capability is by including within your bid information relevant and interesting information about your past projects. Some clients will be quite specific in their requirements. They may request a certain number of examples, requiring specific information about each. A typical request within the bid document may be similar to that shown in Figure 8.1.

Some requests will be quite specific in terms of word count, format and information required. The example in Figure 8.1 just states the minimum information requirements. To win the bid you would need to provide more than the minimum requested in order to stand out from your competitors. Never be satisfied with providing the bare minimum.

Experience			
Please describe your experience in the last THREE years of providing services or works similar to those being sought under this contract. A minimum of the following should be provided for each project:			
Name of client	Brief description of project	Start/end dates	Contract value (£)

FIGURE 8.1: Typical example of a question within tender documentation requesting basic details of experience

Sometimes a question within the bid document will ask for more specific details about your past projects, which may include:

- the main challenges of the project
- the added value that you brought to the project
- examples of innovation
- design awards
- photographs of the finished project.

The key point is to make sure that your answer is compliant, in that you answer the question being asked and give all the information requested. This seems obvious, but it is so easy to be sidetracked into providing information simply because it is available rather than the information actually requested or required. If there are no constraints on your answer, then use this opportunity to show off your talents and skills. You can do this by incorporating a range of project information, which, depending on format and possible constraints such as page or word limit, could include project stamps, mini project profiles, project profiles and case studies.

The need for a knowledge bank

In order to have all the information necessary to prepare a bid at your fingertips, you need to have a good knowledge bank.

The more successful firms will have in place a system for collecting information about their projects as it becomes available. This will include information gathered during the design or construction as well as on completion. Unfortunately, many, less well-organised firms will try to gather information at the last minute. This has numerous disadvantages, including the following:

- the key people may have left the business, so information may be lost
- memory is not as good at the end of the project, or possibly years later. Better quality and more detailed information is easier to gather at the time
- there may be insufficient time to obtain client endorsements
- it is too late to take pictures of key events during construction that might be useful either for a full case study or to address specific issues.

It is far better to create a knowledge bank, which is built up over time, as projects are secured and completed. This knowledge bank should be as comprehensive as possible. It is easier to edit information than to go looking for additional facts many years after a project has been completed. Once in place, the knowledge bank can be used to create a variety of material and can help to populate the firm's website and newsletters as well as the project profiles.

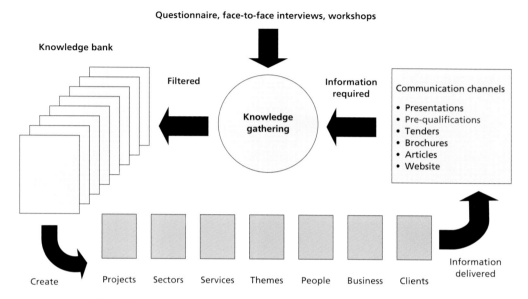

FIGURE 8.2: Creating the knowledge bank

The knowledge-gathering process could be as shown in Figure 8.2. It is advisable that, once a project is commissioned, the person responsible for the task then completes a questionnaire, setting out the key facts about the project. This can be amended and updated during the project and fully updated on project completion. A typical internal project questionnaire is shown in Figure 8.3.

When putting together your project questionnaire, it might be useful to go through all your recent bids and look at the questions that were asked. There may be some recurring themes or topics. For example, in Figure 8.3 you will see that reference is made to collaboration, value engineering and partnering. These topics may have appeared frequently in bids and therefore it is beneficial to include them in the questionnaire to make sure the information is captured. Other topics may include sustainability and building information modelling (BIM) or may be more sector or client specific. From your research you will need to know:

- what is important to your target client
- what are the key issues in the sector
- the sector or client jargon and use that language to demonstrate that you are familiar with the sector.

Project profile questionnaire
Part A: Base information
Name of client:
Name of project:
Project location:
Project value:
Project start and finish dates:
Contract type:
Service provided:
Project description:
Part B: The team
Our team:
Other team members:
Part C: Additional information
Key additional facts:
Challenges of the project:
Added value delivered:
Lessons learned:
Any examples of partnering, collaboration, value engineering, etc?
Part D: Marketing information
Any press coverage? If so, attach
Any awards? If so, attach details
Any photographs? If so, attach
Do we have client's permission to use the project profile?
Do we have client testimonials/endorsement? If so, attach

FIGURE 8.3: A typical internal project questionnaire

Once you have gathered this specific information, you will be able to include it in your project details to add credibility to your experience and skills.

Information from the knowledge bank can also be used to serve the various opportunities that arise for securing projects. These include:

- **the beauty parade** – where you are presenting your capability and experience face to face, usually in competition, to win an assignment and could be during the shortlisting stage
- **the best solution** – this could be a post-bid or post-proposal pitch, where the presenters aim to convince the client that they have the best solution, idea or design
- **speculative 'fishing trip'** – where you attempt to elicit from the client their needs, likes and dislikes and what they intend to purchase in the future
- a presentation addressing a problem set by the client who is looking for **ideas and options** – this might entail reporting on findings and aiming to get the client to commit to further work or the implementation of the recommendations
- **a good idea** – where the presenting team have come up with an idea which may be of interest to the client. This would be a speculative approach.

The use of project stamps, mini project profiles, project profiles and case studies to illustrate a point

Clients will take comfort from seeing that those bidding for work can demonstrate that they have:

- relevant experience
- worked in the same sector
- tackled the same size of project
- good client endorsements
- been seen to be proactive
- been innovative when required.

Nothing will better demonstrate your ability than placing case studies or project profiles or, if appropriate, project stamps and mini project profiles within your submission.

Project stamp

When reading bid documentation, the reader will most likely scan the document first. If the document is set out in a format that is:

- easy to follow and understand
- delivering 'chunks of information'
- seen to be addressing the questions with relevant information

then the reader/evaluator will be in a receptive frame of mind and is more likely to award a higher score than if confronted with pages full of text with no illustrations to complement the points being made.

If space within the bid document is limited, or if you wish to illustrate your experience and capability with reference to several examples, then consider using project stamps.

A project stamp is used to break up the body of the text to incorporate proof of experience and capability.

The project stamp would usually be a key illustration with no more than 20 words of text (see Figure 8.4).

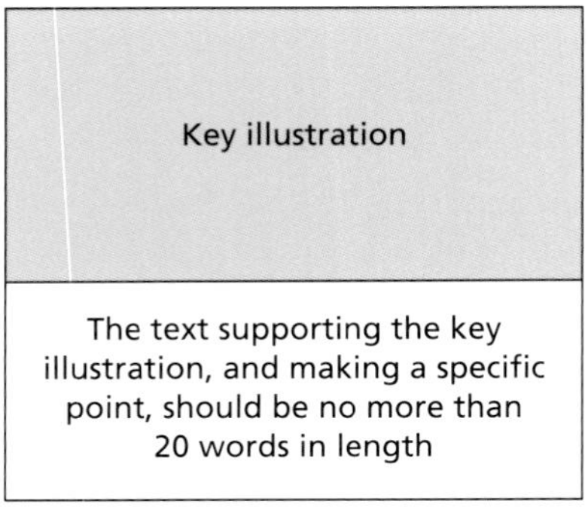

Key illustration

The text supporting the key illustration, and making a specific point, should be no more than 20 words in length

FIGURE 8.4: Format for the project stamp

Mini project profile

A mini project profile is bigger than a project stamp and would probably include:

- the project title and client name
- a brief outline of the assignment, features and benefits, possibly in bullet point format.

A mini project profile is still small enough to be incorporated within the body of the main text (see Figure 8.5 for an example) and gives a few more facts than the project stamp.

Project profile

If more space is available or a specific project is being referred to in the text, then a project profile should be considered. To avoid breaking up the flow of the main text, consider placing project profiles in an appendix or at the end of the relevant section.

Project profiles are also a very useful means of reinforcing the experience listed within team members' CVs. This is especially useful if several members of the team have experience on the same project.

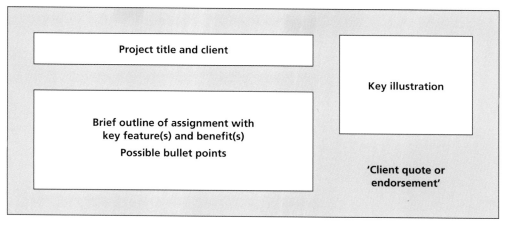

FIGURE 8.5: Format for mini project profile

The project profile should contain:

- the project title and client's name
- key headline facts
- an outline of the assignment or project
- what was delivered and how (features)
- the added value that you brought to the project (benefits)
- key illustration(s)
- a client quote or endorsement.

See Figure 8.6 for an example of a project profile.

Case study

A full case study would include the following, in addition to what is contained in a project profile:

- more detail on the elements outlined for a mini case study or project profile
- the methodology employed on the project
- further explanation of anything innovative or unusual within the project
- commentary from other members of the supply chain/team (clients, consultants or specialist subcontractors).

A full case study is used to show how a specific approach, process or methodology was used that could be transferred to the project for which you are currently bidding. The case study comprises several pages and expands on the highlights contained within the one-page project profile.

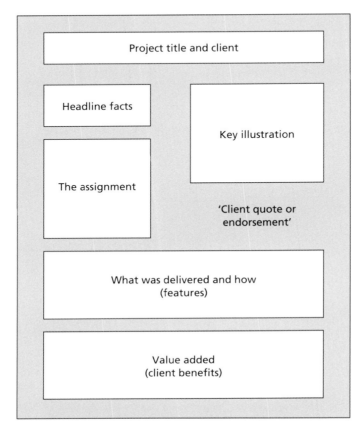

FIGURE 8.6: Format for project profile

A case study could also be harvested for information. If a smaller extract is required, to support a particular point, then the case study could contain that information.

A case study is often used for a landmark project or a project that has something distinctive or innovative about it.

The size or length of case studies would be determined by:

- any constraints imposed by the client on document size or format
- whether the case study is being placed in the body of the text or as an appendix. It is better to use mini project profiles within the main submission and refer to case studies within an appendix
- the style of the rest of the documentation
- the importance of the case study in proving a point
- the number of case studies being used.

Format and content

As a guide:

- a project stamp would be about one-third of an A4 page
- a mini project profile could be one-quarter to half an A4 page
- a project profile would be one page of A4
- a full case study would be several A4 pages long.

It is amazing how little information is kept by professionals and contractors about the work they have done. They always seem to be too busy to keep appropriate records. If the information is gathered as the project proceeds, then appropriate marketing material can be created incorporating facts at a later date. It is almost impossible to write interesting copy without a good sprinkling of facts.

Not all businesses can afford full-time marketing people to keep on top of the fact-gathering exercise. Even if a marketing professional is employed, they will often have to rely on the team members to provide the information.

The easiest way to resolve this problem is to make it part of the procedure that the job cannot be closed down or archived until all the key information is gathered. Key staff may move on or retire and with them goes the specific project knowledge. So, create a system or culture for harvesting project information during the course of the project lifetime.

It is useful to create information in varying lengths so you have ready-made copy to suit all eventual needs. Such copy would include:

- a paragraph summarising the project
- several paragraphs that can be pasted into a document to give an outline of the project
- a project sheet, which would be A4 size (landscape or portrait), incorporating illustrations
- a case study, which could be several pages long, giving a more detailed explanation of the project.

Armed with the above information, you will be able to demonstrate to the client that you are able to undertake their project. But you must be prepared to be very selective and even rewrite project profiles to suit the project you hope to secure.

Write about the key features and resulting benefits

If there is a particular aspect which is very important in the proposed project, then feature that aspect in the project profile. Don't dilute the impact by writing about aspects of the project which are secondary or of little relevance. Remember that the client may have many other teams pitching for the project so you need to grab their attention with facts, features and benefits.

Write about issues and features that will be of interest to the potential client, not simply to you or your peer group.

This does take time and effort and, all too often, the busy professional will cobble together information in the hope that some of it will be relevant.

If you have been given a brief, or have made notes during a briefing session, then you must:

- **feature the information in the same order of priority as the client does** – if the client has spent most of the briefing session saying that they want a low-maintenance, energy-efficient building, then don't start off with big chunks of text explaining how quickly a given project in which you were involved was built and how unique the structural solution was
- **use the client's terminology** wherever you can
- **keep your text short and to the point** – make it easy to read and use short sentences or even bullet points. You need to maintain the client's interest
- if appropriate, and of interest, **convert facts to more manageable information**. Rather than giving the acreage, you might say a project was equivalent to so many football pitches. Or if the height is a key feature why not show the project against a well-known landmark, such as Nelson's Column or the Eiffel Tower.

▶ **SUMMARY CHECKLIST**

◆ Put in place a system to gather facts and figures about your projects

◆ Create a project questionnaire to obtain project details

◆ Use your project details to show off your skills, experience and capability

◆ Comply with the question being asked. If possible add more information, making sure it is still relevant

◆ Use project stamps and mini project profiles to break up the text in order to make it more interesting, relevant and easy to understand

◆ Place project profiles or case studies at the end of the section or in the appendix

◆ Select relevant projects to suit the client's project and to reinforce the experience in the team's CVs, if they are being submitted

◆ In the project profiles, set out the key challenges of the project, how you were able to achieve the required results and the subsequent benefits to the client

◆ Include client quotes and endorsements

◆ Make the text interesting. Don't use long, complex sentences

◆ Use photographs to show the relevant aspects of your projects

CHAPTER 9
Other considerations

Incorporating third party endorsements

Third party endorsements or testimonials are among the most powerful forms of proof you can offer a prospective client about your ability to deliver their project. Clients are reassured by hearing from your other clients just how competent and reliable you are. These endorsements should be used within:

- tenders and proposals
- case studies and project sheets
- brochures
- your website.

In fact, they can be used wherever you want to prove the point you are making.

The best way to obtain a third party endorsement is to ask for it. This request could be part of a feedback questionnaire or be a specific request.

If you have client feedback reviews, then include a request for an endorsement. However, a word of caution here: don't just ask your client for their view of your service because they will probably give you a very general comment, such as:

'I found Wren Barry Architects very professional and they did a very good job for us.'

Having a collection of general comments, however complimentary, is not going to be sufficient. The best approach is to ask your client to comment on certain aspects of your service. The client might even ask you to prepare a draft for modification. This has the following benefits:

- the endorsement praises specific aspects that are relevant
- it saves the client the time and trouble of thinking what to say
- a single endorsement can be used for several different aspects of your service and the project.

Consider how you will use the endorsement

When obtaining third party endorsements, consider how you will use them. You may want to show that you have relevant experience, have provided a good service and possess a whole range of specific skills. So take some time to prepare a list of things that a prospective client might want to know. This might vary from sector to sector or with building type. Take a look at past tenders or bids and identify which questions the clients ask most frequently. Are there recurring themes?

Let's assume that Wren Barry Architects have just finished the design of a school and are now looking for client endorsements that could be used to help win future bids. After some consideration, they have decided that they want endorsements to show their strengths in the following areas:

- liaising with the client
- working well with the project stakeholders
- taking the client through the design process
- understanding current school design requirements
- being innovative
- being a pleasure to work with
- working well with other consultants and the building contractor
- being able to accommodate change
- being proficient project managers once on site and competent contract administrators
- helping the school to use the project as a learning tool for their students.

Therefore, Wren Barry Architects could perhaps send a letter to the headmaster along these lines:

Dear Mr Jones

New Science Block

It was good to see you again last Thursday at the official opening of the new science block. I was pleased to hear all the complimentary comments by teachers, students and governors about the new facility.

After the reception you kindly agreed to write a testimonial which we could use within our marketing literature and in future tenders. I know it's always difficult to start with a blank piece of paper and to save you some time I have put together an example of some of the points you might like to cover. Anything along these lines would be appreciated. Feel free to edit it or draft an entirely new one.

You may wish to comment on how we approached the following aspects:

- *liaising with you, the teachers, student representatives and the governors*
- *taking you through the design process*

- *understanding your needs for a new science block*
- *being innovative*
- *working well with other consultants and the building contractor*
- *the changing brief and our ability to accommodate change*
- *project managing once on site and contract administration*
- *using the project as a learning tool for your students.*

Please let me know if you wish me to elaborate on any of the above and I look forward to your response in due course.

Yours sincerely

From this we might expect something on the lines of:

Sample testimonial

Dean Bridge School appointed Wren Barry Architects to design their new science block. The contract sum was £3.25 million.

From the outset Joe Henderson, the Wren Barry Architects project architect, became very involved and worked closely with all the teachers, student representatives and governors to develop a brief for our new science block. This was, for many of us, our first building project and Joe talked us through the design process and guided us through the decision-making process. Although our wish list was long, we found that Wren Barry Architects helped us to prioritise our requirements so we were able to obtain maximum value from our limited budget.

We found that working with Wren Barry Architects had the extra benefit that they were very experienced in designing science blocks. They arranged visits to some of their past projects and we were able to talk to their other clients and found this reassuring. Due to their experience, we found that Wren Barry Architects were introducing some innovative ideas that we had not considered but we felt that they were so beneficial that we incorporated them.

We also appointed several other consultants and Wren Barry Architects were able to coordinate their input into the project and acted as our single point of contact. This, we found, cut down substantially on the administration, for which we are thankful. Wren Barry Architects continued to project manage the contract once on site and we found that the whole team, including the contractor, was working in harmony for the benefit of the project.

Finally, I would like to thank Joe Henderson for giving up so much of his own time to get involved in helping our staff create a teaching module which ran in conjunction with the design of the project and then during its construction. I am pleased to say that several of our students have since indicated their interest in a career within the construction industry.

Yours sincerely

This endorsement might seem to be long, but the idea is that it can be harvested for a number of quotes to cover many different requirements, as shown below.

Given the endorsement above, you would be able to produce quotes to incorporate within bid documents along the lines of:

Involving stakeholders

'From the outset Joe Henderson, the Wren Barry Architects project architect, became very involved and worked closely with all the teachers, student representatives and governors to develop a brief for our new science block.'

Ability to explain the process

'This was, for many of us, our first building project and Joe talked us through the design process and guided us through the decision-making process.'

Maximum value for limited budget

'Although our wish list was long, we found that Wren Barry Architects helped us to prioritise our requirements so we were able to obtain maximum value from our limited budget.'

And so on, for innovative approach, team coordination and other aspects of the project.

In addition, a request to the other consultants involved in the project covering technical issues could generate further endorsements on points such as:

- taking a proactive approach to resolving problems
- driving the team to produce a high-quality building
- taking great care to reduce the carbon footprint of the project
- being open to ideas from other consultants that could result in a building that offers better value for money.

From this single project it can be seen that it is possible to generate many useful quotes as endorsements for future use. Ensuring that you follow this process for every project will result in a whole library of endorsements to prove a variety of claims that you may make in your bids and proposals.

Always review your endorsements to make sure that questions that are currently being asked at the tender and pre-qualification stage are covered. If new issues start to arise, then incorporate these within your requests to clients when seeking endorsements.

Supplying client references

During the course of the pre-qualification stage you may be asked to supply several client references. You will be asked for the contact details of one or more clients who could be contacted directly for feedback on their thoughts on your suitability for the project under consideration.

When providing contacts bear in mind the following caveats:

- don't give out the details of the same client as a contact too frequently; they might not take kindly to being constantly inundated with requests for information
- obtain your client's permission to be used as a reference client
- alert your clients to the fact that they might be contacted in respect of a certain project for which you are bidding
- talk through the project that you are pitching for with your client and ask them if they would be good enough to highlight certain qualities in your service delivery. These qualities will be those that you have identified as being important to the prospective client.

Using CVs

The client will want to know who will be working on their assignment, should you be successful in your bid. The most common way to provide such information within a bid is to include CVs. The various formats are detailed below:

CV link stamp or icon	This is similar to the project stamp in size (see Chapter 8) and will include a face portrait and a few words giving name, position in the firm and role within the project. Although not a CV in itself, it can be used to identify a key person within the bid documents and provide a link to the full CV, which may appear in the appendix (see Figure 9.1).
Mini profile or pen portrait	This is similar to the mini project profile in size and will be used to summarise the person's career, skills and role within the project. This is useful if a full CV is not requested and gives an insight into a person's credentials. Some clients will actually ask for a pen portrait (see Figure 9.2).

Full CV

This is the more traditional format. The CV may be one or more pages long and will show:

- name, profession, specialisation and position in the firm
- career summary and career highlights
- professional qualifications and professional memberships
- résumé.

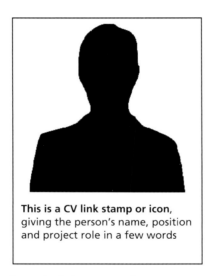

This is a CV link stamp or icon, giving the person's name, position and project role in a few words

FIGURE 9.1: Typical format for a CV link stamp or icon

This is a mini profile or pen portrait

This will highlight the person's key experience and skills.

The pen portrait could include a very brief career overview and perhaps mention a few key projects that are relevant to the current bid.

There may be room to incorporate a quote from a past client praising the person's abilities.

Also, state the key benefit to the project of including this person.

FIGURE 9.2: Typical format for a mini profile or pen portrait

It is important for a firm that is selling professional services to have regularly updated CVs of its team available. There are three basic stages in the development of a CV for inclusion within a bid document. These are:

Stage 1: **base CV**	As each team member completes a project, develops new skills, gains new qualifications or is promoted, this information should be added to their CV.
Stage 2: **sector, building-type** **or skill specific CV**	From the base CV, various specialist CVs can be created. These can be sector specific or cover just one building type or a particular skill set. The main point is that the client will want to see how appropriate the person is for their project; if you are pitching for a new science block at a school you will not want to feature housing projects on the CV.
Stage 3: **bid-specific CV**	When you know the particular requirements of the project for which you are bidding you must modify your most appropriate Stage 2 CVs to reflect the client's needs.

Creating a bid-specific CV

When creating a bid-specific CV you should ask yourself:

- What is the client looking for in their professional team?
- Does the CV show off the appropriate qualities to secure the assignment?
- Are there any additional points that could be included, or might existing elements be restructured to improve the CV and make it more appropriate?

If the bid is for a new science block in a school then do not focus heavily on housing project experience. If the person does not have specific school science block experience, then include other relevant experience, such as similar projects or other projects for schools. If there is no relevant experience then seriously reconsider your chances of being successful.

Use the résumé section, which may be placed at the beginning of the CV, to bring out the specific points that you want the client to notice. Also, to make this more bespoke, mention the client and project within this résumé, as shown in the following example:

Résumé for Joe Henderson

Joe Henderson is a senior project architect with over ten years' experience within the education sector. During this time, Joe has completed four projects that have included the provision of a new science block, similar in size and complexity to that proposed by Dean Bridge School.

On all four projects, Joe has been involved from inception, throughout the design process and during on-site contract administration. This makes Joe particularly suitable for this project. He will be fully aware of the need to liaise with the many stakeholders involved in Dean Bridge School. This will have the added benefit of enabling him to quickly and efficiently take a brief and present initial concept designs for approval.

Joe has a particular interest in sustainable design and his last project was featured in many journals regarding the incorporation of energy-saving elements. We note that this is of particular interest to Dean Bridge School.

To improve your chances of success, always rewrite the CVs and make them as bespoke as possible. Where several CVs are included, make sure that they are all in the same format (which might be specified by the client). This is particularly important if you are teaming up with external consultants.

Using an experience or skills matrix

If the project is large or complex, then the client will probably want to be reassured that your proposed team has all the relevant experience and skills. In this situation the inclusion of an experience or skills matrix will be a useful addition to your portfolio of CVs. This

Skills	Team members			
	Hugh Barry	Joe Henderson	Sue Warden	John Gilmore
Brief taking	✓	✓		
Concept design	✓	✓	✓	
Stakeholder workshops and liaison	✓	✓		
Detailed design	✓	✓	✓	✓
Value engineering		✓		
Contract administration	✓	✓		
Project management	✓	✓		
Interior design			✓	
Landscape design				✓

FIGURE 9.3: Typical layout for a skills matrix

will also enable you to show additional skills and experience that might not have been asked for but could be relevant and might help to differentiate you from the competitors. The example in Figure 9.3 shows a simple typical format.

When using a skills matrix, try to use skills descriptions that the client will understand, especially if they have not identified such a skill requirement in the bid documents. In the example shown in Figure 9.3 the client might not know what is meant by 'value engineering' or 'stakeholder workshops and liaison'. Therefore you may need to explain within the submission what these skills are and their consequent client benefits.

▶ SUMMARY CHECKLIST
• Incorporate client endorsements within your bid
• Make the endorsements relevant to the topic
• Provide past clients with guidance on the points to cover in their endorsements
• Create a database of endorsements under specific topics and attributes
• When providing client contact details for references, always brief the client to expect a call. Also, request that they highlight particular aspects of your service if given the opportunity
• Create a comprehensive CV for each of your team members
• From the base CV, create sector, skill or building-type specific CVs
• For every bid opportunity, rewrite the CVs so they become truly bespoke
• Make sure that the format and content of CVs comply with any instructions within the bid documents
• Include a skills or experience matrix if appropriate

Index

added value/benefits 19–20, 29
additional services 60, 61
appendices 59, 83–8

bid / no bid evaluation 38, 57
bid team 14–15, 53
bid/proposal documentation 63–82
    appendices 59, 83–8
    executive summary 75
    format and production 57–61, 71
    lists, tables and graphics 80–1
    preparation process 54–6
    using the client's language 70–3
    writing from the client's point of view
        73–4
bid/proposal preparation
    achieving success 2–3, 39–40
    demonstrating capability 30–1, 36
    demonstrating compatibility 31–4, 37,
        50, 70–1
    establishing credibility 14, 27–9, 36,
        63–5
    establishing reliability 34, 37
    as the incumbent provider 45–7
    process 54–6
    standing out from favourites and
        incumbents 44–5
    timetable 53, 55
bid/proposal selection process 18–19
    (see also evaluation criteria)

capability, demonstrating 30–1, 36
case studies 14, 95–6
client references 105
clients (see also projects)
    approach to procurement 16–17

demonstrating compatibility with 31–4,
    37, 50, 70–1
external advisers/consultants 17, 21
feedback from 34–7
key contacts 21–2, 71–3
language and point of view 70–4
lines of communication 24
programme/schedule 15–16
project selection 13–15, 38–9, 57
relationship with 23–4, 31–3, 38–9,
    53–4
collaborative working 7–8, 33
compatibility, demonstrating 31–4, 37, 50,
    70–1
competitors 17, 43–52
    analysis of 47–8
    differentiating from 49–51, 60
    favourites and incumbents 43–5
consultants see external advisers/experts/
    consultants
contractor bids 8–10
credibility, demonstrating 14, 27–9, 36,
    63–5
customer service 44–5, 50–1, 65–6
CVs 105–9

debriefing 35–6
delivery team 31, 53, 59
design and build contracts 8–10
documentation 90–7 (see also
    bid/proposal documentation; tender
    documentation)

e-auctions 11
e-procurement 10–11
European Union (EU) procedures 3–4

evaluation criteria
  clients' 18–19, 40, 63
  project selection 38, 57
executive summaries 75
expertise 14–15, 31, 108–9
expression of interest (EOI) 4
external advisers/experts/consultants
  for bid preparation 15, 108
  clients' 17, 21

feedback from clients 34–7
fees 7, 21, 60
framework contracts/agreements 6–7
funding, project 20

graphics 80–1

incumbent providers 44–7
invitation to tender (ITT) 4

key contacts 21–2, 71–3
knowledge bank 90–7

negotiated contracts 5, 6
novation 8–9

open tender process 6

past projects *see* track record
personnel *see* resources
pre-qualification questionnaire (PQQ) 4, 47
previous projects *see* track record
procurement agencies 11
procurement approach 16–17
procurement programme/schedule 15–16
project profiles 14, 92, 94–6
project stamps 93–4
projects 13–21 (*see also* clients)
  bid selection / evaluation criteria 18–19,
    40, 63
  funding and estimated value 20–1
  previous 14, 30, 90–7

procurement approach 16–17
procurement programme/schedule 15–16
  selecting suitable 13–15, 38–9, 57
proposals 2, 5, 58–9 (*see also* bid/proposal
  preparation)
public sector procedures 3–4, 5–6

relationship management 23–4, 38–9
reliability, establishing 34, 37
resources
  bid team 14–15, 53
  delivery team 31, 53, 59
  expertise 14–15, 31, 108–9
restricted tender process 5
risk-avoidance 50

schedules *see* timetable
selection process 18–19 (*see also*
  evaluation criteria)
service delivery 44–5, 50–1, 65–6, 69–70
skills matrix 108–9
storyboards 58
subcontractor bids 8–10
supporting documentation 83–8
SWOT analysis 48–9

team bids 7–8
team meetings 55
team members 105–9
team working 7–8, 33
tender documentation
  bias 43
  examining 54–5, 69
testimonials 14, 101–5
third party assessment (TPA) 46
third party endorsements 14, 101–5
timetable
  bid preparation 53, 55
  procurement 15–16
track record 14, 30, 89–99
  competitors' 44
two-stage tender 4